CHANCE

Mother and Father, 1930s Warsaw, before the war

Uri Shulevitz

Escape from the Holocaust

Farrar Straus Giroux
New York

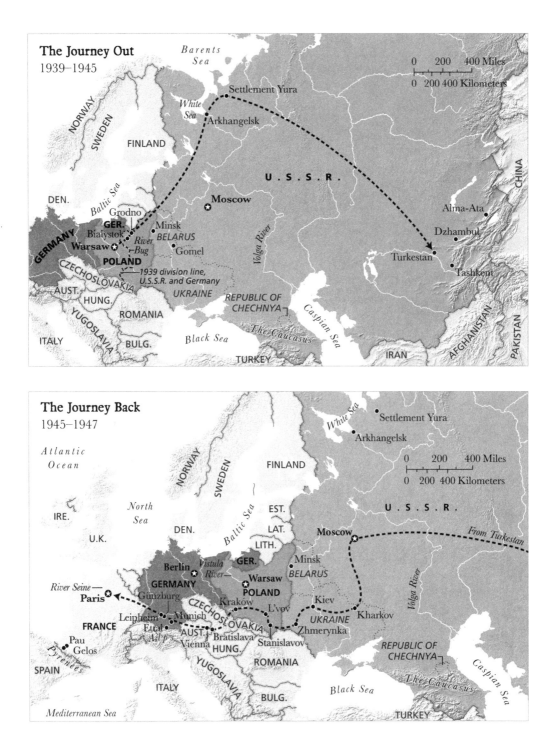

The Journey Out
1939–1945

Barents Sea

NORWAY

SWEDEN

White Sea

Settlement Yura

Arkhangelsk

FINLAND

Baltic Sea

0   200   400 Miles

0   200 400 Kilometers

U.S.S.R.

DEN.

Grodno

GER.

Bialystok

Minsk

Moscow

Alma-Ata

Dzhambul

GERMANY

River Bug

BELARUS

Warsaw

POLAND

Gomel

Volga River

Turkestan

Tashkent

CZECHOSLOVAKIA

1939 division line,
U.S.S.R. and Germany

AUST.

HUNG.

UKRAINE

REPUBLIC OF CHECHNYA

Caspian Sea

CHINA

ROMANIA

YUGOSLAVIA

The Caucasus

ITALY

BULG.

Black Sea

TURKEY

IRAN

AFGHANISTAN

PAKISTAN

The Journey Back
1945–1947

Atlantic Ocean

White Sea

Settlement Yura

Arkhangelsk

NORWAY

SWEDEN

FINLAND

EST.

U.S.S.R.

IRE.

North Sea

DEN.

Baltic Sea

LAT.

LITH.

Moscow

From Turkestan

U.K.

Minsk

BELARUS

Volga River

Berlin

Vistula River

GER.

River Seine

GERMANY

Warsaw

Paris

Günzburg

POLAND

Kiev

Kharkov

FRANCE

Leipheim

Kraków

L'vov

UKRAINE

Ettal

Munich

CZECHOSLOVAKIA

Alps

AUST.

Bratislava

Zhmerynka

Pau

Gelos

Vienna

HUNG.

Stanislavov

REPUBLIC OF CHECHNYA

Pyrénées

The Caucasus

SPAIN

ITALY

YUGOSLAVIA

ROMANIA

Caspian Sea

BULG.

Black Sea

Mediterranean Sea

TURKEY

0   200   400 Miles

0   200 400 Kilometers

CONTENTS

ONE
WARSAW

I

On September 1, 1939, Nazi planes burst into the Warsaw skies, some dropping incendiary bombs and spreading fires throughout the city, others dropping high-explosive bombs and turning buildings into dust.

Nature responded with heavy rains angrily pound-
ing the pavement.

Terrified people ran in all directions.

Streets were ripped into deep canyons.

Faucets ran dry. Between bombings, people dragged heavy buckets of water from the Vistula River for drinking and cooking.

Smoke from the fires painted everything gray. Not far from our building, amid this grayness, were big mounds of brilliant pigments—reds, yellows, blues—in the courtyard of a paint factory in ruins.

I watched from our window in a daze. I didn't fully realize what I was seeing, although it was all happening right in front of my eyes. It seemed unreal and distant.

Later that day, I sat on a table, and as Mother was  putting a pair of new boots on my feet, she said, "We'll need to walk a lot."

I was four years old.

2

For days, as the bombs fell, my mother and I stayed inside. Although the doors and windows were tightly shut, a noise from hell filled every room of our small apartment. The terrifying whistling of gunfire and explosions of bombs was unbearable.

My only refuge was drawing. Always drawing, drawing, drawing. I drew stick figures. Stick figures marching back and forth on pieces of Father's old newspapers, filling up any empty space on the page I could find.

Each time I heard an explosion, I closed my eyes and held the paper in the air. Now my pencil became an airplane, flying at top speed, point first, piercing round holes into the paper.

It became a game of chance. *Will the stick figures evade*

that frightful pencil-plane? Will they be hit? Will we be hit? Are we going to die? Will we starve to death?

Our food was almost gone. Mother decided to go down to buy bread. In these uncertain, unpredictable days, she didn't want to leave me alone in the apartment. So I went with her.

When we came out to the dark hallway and headed toward the stairs, what I saw took my breath away.

The staircase had a large gaping hole all the way through it, from top to bottom.

On each floor, a narrow wooden plank made an improvised bridge over the hole to the next floor, wide enough to walk up or down but too narrow to cover the hole completely.

I said, "I'm scared. I'm not going down."

Mother said, "We must. With no food we'll grow weak. We must be strong and brave. I'm not leaving you alone!"

I had no choice. There was no arguing with Mother.

Running down the stairs used to be a game; now it was a nightmare. Trembling, I cautiously followed Mother down the rickety planks. It was impossible not to look off to the sides, into the crater. Seeing the hole made me dizzy.

I had to stop periodically to regain my balance.

Before the war, Father once took me to the Warsaw Zoo. I never forgot the hippo that opened its mouth to yawn, revealing what looked to me like a deep cave with two teeth as large as butcher blocks.

I was blessed with, or perhaps cursed by, a vivid imagination.

Now, walking down the wooden planks, I was

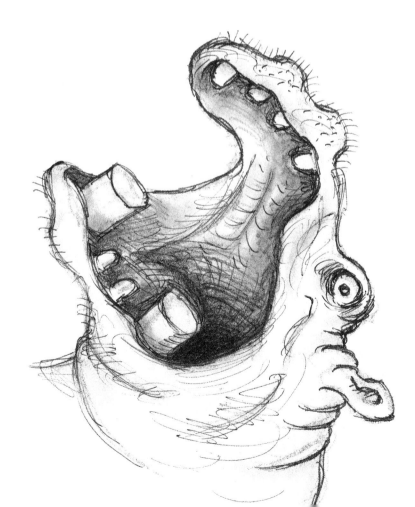

convinced that I'd be swallowed up by that hole—the hole that looked to me like the hippo's gaping mouth. If that happened, I knew I would be chewed up by huge butcher-block teeth and would die a horrible death.

But I made it downstairs.

When I finally reached the courtyard alive, it was a great relief.

While Mother waited in a breadline, I stood off to the side.

Older kids collected empty bullet casings and pieces of shrapnel in the rubble, as if it were all a game.

My relief was short-lived.

Suddenly, there was a sharp whistling sound followed by

an **EXPLOSION!**

Thick dust and smoke filled
the courtyard. I couldn't
see anything.

When the smoke settled . . .

some people who a second
ago had been standing on the
breadline lay dead; others
lay wounded. It all seemed
unreal. Dazed, I watched,
frozen in place. The distance
between life and death had
vanished. One second life, the
next death.

A miracle: Mother was unhurt.

4

Even before the air raid, contradictory rumors had run wild in Warsaw. It was difficult, or impossible, to know the truth. One rumor that started circulating was that the invaders were going to mobilize all the men for slave labor. True or not, many young men left Warsaw as a result. Father had decided to leave Warsaw as well.

Mother and I remained behind and endured the air raid without Father. The plan was to join him later.

After Father left, Mother seemed worried. So I, too, began to worry. *What is going to happen to us?*

Each time I looked at Mother's sad, anxious face, I worried even more. I didn't ask questions: I was too afraid of the answers. Mother had no answers anyway.

She wasn't alone. No one had answers.

Then some people came after the Nazi attack and told Mother they had heard that, after leaving Warsaw, Father was killed in an air raid.

5

Four years earlier, when

I was brought home from the hospital, my parents had not yet decided on a name
for me. Then Father noticed that as I lay in my
crib, I was staring intently at the flowers on the
wallpaper.

Father said to Mother, "I think our little son
will be an artist. His name should be Uri, after
the biblical Uri, father of Bezalel, the first artist
of the Bible." Mother agreed. So I became Uri.

Little did I know how by chance my name would save our lives.

As soon as I could hold a pencil, I got busy proving Father right. I began decorating the walls of our apartment with scribbles. When I graduated from scribbling on the walls, I began to draw stick figures on the margins of Father's newspapers.

No matter where my stick figures were going, right or left, back or forth, they always looked straight out. One day, Mother said, "Figures don't always look straight out at us. Sometimes they look to the side because they have a profile."

Profile? Who had ever heard of such a thing? What a revelation! I asked Mother to show me how to do a profile.

She took a piece of my newsprint and showed me. "First you draw a circle for the head. Then you draw a small potato for the nose. You attach the potato to the circle. Next you add a dot for an eye, and then you have a profile."

This was too exciting for words! From then on, I made sure that all my stick figures, no matter where they went, right or left, back or forth, were always in profile.

And so began my artistic career.

6

Before the war, I had two big concerns.

One: "Did Napoleon have a beard?"

I'd heard Father talking to family friends about the French emperor Napoleon, who had conquered much of Europe more than a century before. Napoleon—who had ever heard such a mysterious, fascinating name? From then on, I couldn't stop thinking about him and what he might have looked like.

"No," Mother said, "Napoleon didn't have a beard."

Two: "Does the world have an end?"

I reasoned that the world must be like a dish, but a little bigger. So when I grew up, I'd go to the end of the world and look over the edge to see what was going on down below.

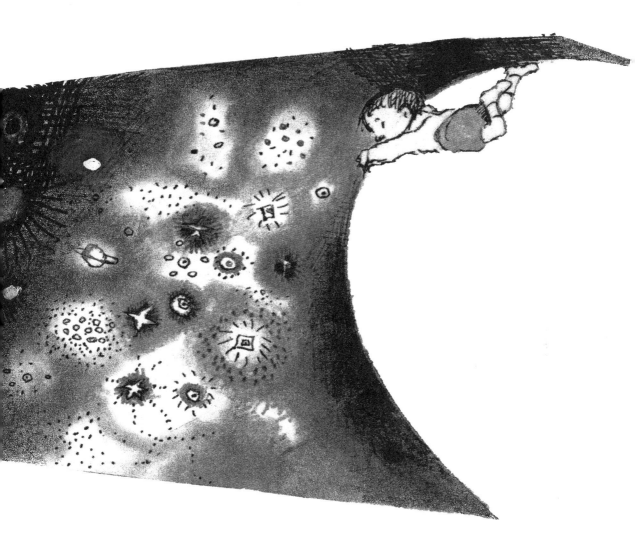

I told Father my plans.

"No," Father explained, "the world has no end, because it's shaped like an egg, not like a dish."

When the war came, everything changed. I no longer had two concerns. Only one: how to survive.

7

Father wasn't dead.

Contrary to rumors, he had managed to leave Poland and make it to Bialystok, which had been part of Poland before the war but was now a part of the Soviet Union.

Father was one of thousands of refugees who had fled Poland. Bialystok was flooded with more new refugees every day. As a result, there was a tremendous lack of housing and work.

Father was lucky. By chance he found a place to stay, and because he had worked in Warsaw for an ice-cream factory, painting all its signs and decorating its trucks, he found work painting Soviet slogans on banners.

Many refugees were unhappy with the conditions

in Bialystok and decided to return to Nazi-occupied Poland. In spite of his luck—having both work and housing—Father wasn't happy. He felt lonely. He missed his family, and he wondered if he'd made the right decision to leave his family behind, so he, too, decided to return to Warsaw.

8

Crossing the border had become more difficult. Father took the train from Bialystok to a small town on the Soviet-Polish border. From the train station, he walked to an abandoned warehouse. The warehouse had a hole in the back, which people crawled through in order to sneak across the border. Just as Father was about to crawl from the Soviet side

to the Polish side, a young Jewish man crawled in from the Polish side.

He looked very frightened.

When he saw Father, he asked, "Are you Jewish?"

Father nodded.

"Are you trying to return to Nazi-occupied Poland?" the young man asked.

Father said, "Yes. I've left a wife and a young son, and the rest of my family."

The young man looked at him, stunned. "Have you lost your mind? Do you want to return to the hell from which I just escaped? Tell your wife and child to come join you here." He grabbed Father's arm and said, "Come, let's take the train to Bialystok," then forcibly dragged him to the train station. He said, "Someday you'll thank me for my advice."

9

Had Father not been stopped from returning to Nazi-occupied Poland and joining the rest of our family, our fate would have been the same as theirs: death.

Some may say: "It was pure chance that he tried to leave the Soviet Union at exactly the same time as the young man was entering."

Others, with a religious outlook, may claim that it wasn't chance, but divine intervention: "The young man was sent by God to stop him from returning to Poland."

But why would divine intervention have saved my parents' lives when they were not religious? Why, then, did my devout grandfather die a miserable death at the hands of the Nazis, when he was a deeply religious man who observed every single commandment of his faith with love and devotion? Why was he not saved by divine intervention?

I have no answers.

10

There was a clandestine underground mail
service that smuggled the refugees' mail between Bialystok and Warsaw. Father used the service to write to
Mother and ask her to come join him.

When Mother received Father's letter, we were overjoyed. Father was alive!

During the Nazi bombing, we had had a fire in one
of the rooms in our apartment. Mother packed a small
bundle of what was left: a blanket, two sheets, a couple
of photographs, and a few articles of clothing.

When it came time for our departure, Mother's
sister and brother and her brother's children came to
say good-bye. Her brother said, "Please don't leave.
We've heard of the frightening conditions of the refugees in Bialystok: the overcrowding, the lack of work
and housing. Tell your husband to come back here.

Whatever our fate will be, at least our family will be together."

His children were crying and begging him to let them go with Mother. He refused.

Mother was determined to join Father in Bialystok. She wouldn't change her mind.

Mother (at right) with sister Bronia

I I

Mother reserved a place for us on a smugglers' truck. The night before our departure we hardly slept. A hesitant morning came at last, as if the night were reluctant to open its eyes and gaze upon a world in ruin.

A light rain fell. It was still partly dark. We sat in the open back of a truck on long, hard benches, a row of gloomy, worried faces. We were apprehensive of what was to come. I sat next to Mother, trembling from the chill and fear. We all sat in silence. Occasionally some-

one spoke in a hushed whisper. We had no wish to call attention to ourselves.

After riding for a while, we passed by Polish road workers, repairing the road damaged by the Nazi bombardments. When they saw us, they stopped work and called out, *"Żydzi do Palestyny!"* ("Jews, go to Palestine!")

Had they forgotten who their true enemies were?

So much for being unnoticed.

12

Somehow we managed to leave Warsaw without being stopped. I don't remember how long we rode on the smugglers' truck. At some point the truck stopped near a wooded area. The smugglers told us that was as far as they could go without getting into trouble. They gave us directions to the eastern border.

And so began the long walk that Mother had predicted. At first through woods, then through fields, and finally on a road leading to the River Bug (pronounced *Boog*). The river was the new border between Nazi-occupied Poland and Soviet-occupied Poland. Just before the invasion of Poland by the Nazis, the Soviet Union and Germany had signed a pact, agreeing not to attack each other. After the invasion, as part of that agreement, the Soviet Union took over parts of eastern Poland.

It was early in the Nazi occupation of Poland, and the systematic roundups of Jews hadn't yet begun. The border was still open. Soldiers on both sides let us go through. In fact, a young soldier from the regular German army patted me on the head and gave me a candy. Later on, I might've gotten a bullet instead.

After crossing the border, we were now in Soviet Belarus. More walking followed, to a train station, and a train that eventually got us to Bialystok.

I didn't complain throughout the journey, but once in Bialystok, I fell ill from stress and fatigue.

TWO

BIALYSTOK

I

When we first arrived in Bialystok, we and the rest of a group of refugees were welcomed by a young Russian soldier who praised the wonders of the Soviet regime.

He said, "In the Soviet Union, we have plenty of everything. We have tea and we even have sugar."

Both were such luxuries in those days.

When one of us asked, "Do you have lemons for tea?" he declared, "Sure, we do. They're just now building a lemon factory."

At first it looked like the soldier was right. The store windows in Bialystok were full of all kinds of delicious-looking food: sausages and other meats, bread loaves and rolls, vegetables and fruits. But when we entered the store and asked to buy what we saw in the window, we were always told, "Sorry, it's been sold out."

Later we found out that all the beautiful food we saw stuffed in the store windows was made of wood or plaster, painted in appealing colors.

2

While I was ill, my parents befriended a fellow Jewish refugee from Poland. His young son, Hayim Genelde, was around nine years old and already an accomplished poet. He wrote long poems in rhyme. Mother introduced him to me. While I was sick in bed, he came to entertain me. He told me stories and recited his poems along with poems by other poets. And so we became friends, in spite of the age difference. I was just four years old, and, being an only child, I looked up to him like the older brother I wished I had. I was so proud to have such a friend.

3

Since Polish and Russian are both Slavic languages, with many similarities, it is fairly easy for a Polish speaker to pick up Russian, the main language of the Soviet Union. As a four-year-old, I spoke it only two weeks after our arrival in Bialystok. My parents began speaking it not long after.

4

In early 1940, there came an order from the Soviet government in Moscow, the capital, that all refugees must register. We were given a choice: get Soviet citizenship or return to Nazi-occupied Poland. My parents had no desire to return to the Nazis, so they decided to apply for Soviet citizenship.

Father's job was painting banners at the state sign-making cooperative.

As soon as his work allowed, he went to get our citizenship papers. The line was long. After he waited patiently, Father's turn came.

The passport clerk began to fill out the application. He asked Father, "What's your name?"

"Abraham Shulevitz."

"Your wife's name?"

Father told the clerk her name.

"Children?"

"Yes, a four-year-old boy."

"What is his name?"

"Uri."

"Uri!" exclaimed the clerk, and looked at Father with suspicion.

Father asked, "Is there something wrong, Comrade Secretary?" In the communist Soviet Union, where private property wasn't allowed, everyone was called "comrade" as a sign of brotherhood and solidarity.

"Is something wrong?" repeated the clerk. "There's something terribly wrong!"

Father was stunned into silence.

The clerk continued, with an accusatory look: "I know your kind! You've named your son after that Zionist poet Uri Zvi Greenberg. You must be an anti-Soviet reactionary just like him."

When Father recovered his voice, he protested. "Uri

is a biblical name. It has nothing to do with being anti-Soviet."

But as soon as the clerk heard "Uri," Father's words began falling on deaf ears. No passports for us.

When Father returned home, upset from his encounter with the clerk, he told Mother what had happened. After discussing it, they decided not to seek Soviet citizenship.

I never saw the clerk. I only heard Father say that he was a fellow Jew who had found it to his advantage to become a Communist, so I pictured him in my mind with a mustache, because the Soviet leader Comrade Stalin had one, and the clerk's mustache would testify what a loyal Communist he was.

As a result of the exchange with the passport clerk, Father became frightened. What next? He now worried that because of his four-year-old son's name, he would be arrested for being an enemy of the Soviet Union. He had heard about the infamous Soviet show

trials, in which false accusations led to the executions
of innocent people.

5

Lacking Soviet citizenship had its consequences. It required us to stay only in restricted places, far from the border.

The day after Father's visit to the clerk's office, he went back to work at the state sign-making co-op and was told that he was fired because he didn't have Soviet citizenship. Now Father had no work.

He wasn't the only one fired from his job. Many other refugees without Soviet citizenship lost their jobs as well. Among them were talented actors, writers, and directors from Jewish theaters in Poland. So they decided to create a new Jewish theater in Bialystok and to perform in Yiddish. When Father heard about it, he proposed to work for them designing sets. His offer was accepted.

In addition to the actors performing plays and short

skits, famous Jewish singers from Warsaw sang popular Yiddish songs—some of them humorous, others sentimental—that brought tears to the audience's eyes, making them long for the lives and homes they had before the war. The performers played to full houses.

6

After the theater was established, a new director was appointed by Moscow, and the original director became his assistant. Although Father's set-making work was well liked, he was fired once more because he didn't have Soviet citizenship. Others probably lost their jobs for the same reason.

After his dismissal, Father went to the theater director's office to ask for his last paycheck.

The director looked annoyed and said, "We have no money now. When the money comes from Minsk"—the Belarus capital—"you'll get paid."

"Comrade Director," Father said, "I have no money to buy food for my family."

The director said angrily, "Do I need to repeat myself? You'll get paid when the money comes from Minsk."

The director's assistant kindly offered to loan Father money for food from his own pocket.

The director forbade it. "There will be no loans!" he said.

7

After being fired from the Jewish theater, Father went to look for another job in another theater's set-design department. Eventually, he found work with the state theater of the city of Gomel, currently performing in Bialystok. Unlike the Jewish theater, which performed in Yiddish, the Gomel theater performed in Russian.

After a series of successful performances in Bialystok, the theater company planned to perform in the town of Grodno, about a three-hour journey away. The theater's artistic director asked Father to travel with them. When Father left, Mother and I remained in Bialystok.

8

Because of the uncertain times, Father felt
that we should be together, so he sent a letter asking
us to come join him in Grodno as soon as possible. He
had found an apartment for us to stay in.

Day by day, the lives of refugees without Soviet
passports were getting more and more difficult. There
were rumors that the authorities were planning a surprise for them. That meant for us as well, since we had
no Soviet passports.

But we had no idea what that surprise might be.

9

When Mother received Father's letter to come to Grodno, she assumed it would be for a short stay. Since the weather was warm, she wore a cotton dress. She packed a few items and left the rest in Bialystok. Among the belongings left behind were some family photos. One of them I still remember. It was a photo of me at two and a half or three, sitting happily in a sandbox and singing, mouth wide open.

10

After we joined Father in Grodno, Mother made another desperate attempt to convince our relatives to leave Poland and come join us. They refused. She wrote letters pleading to at least send the children. They refused once more.

Mother's brother was very clever, but unfortunately not very wise. We never saw him or his family again.

11

Life in Grodno was more pleasant than in Bialystok. Since there weren't as many refugees, food was more readily available. In the evenings, my parents went to see plays at the theater for free, because Father worked there. During the day, we visited him backstage and watched him work.

On one of our visits backstage, Father showed us the costumes and the sets. I was surprised to see that they were made of paper and cardboard, painted to look real. Being very light, they were easy to transport from city to city when the theater company traveled.

I was most impressed by a miniature model of a scene that Father and other workers were getting ready to build full-scale. It was a landscape with a tree. What I found most fascinating was the hilly ground made up of small pieces of uneven wood of different shapes, over which a piece of thin cloth was stretched. I was amazed at how real the landscape looked. An illusion created by such simple means.

Oh, how I wished then that I could draw that small model! In reality I had not the slightest idea of even how to begin. I had to content myself with my stick figures. Although I could now draw them in profile, I knew that they bore little resemblance to real people. For that, all I needed was to look around me.

I've forgotten much of those long-gone years. But I've never forgotten that small model.

My parents encouraged my every drawing attempt. They praised highly every drawing I made. But even as a very young kid, I knew that my drawings were lacking. My parents' compliments were okay, but what I yearned for most was more help and tips on how to improve my drawings.

12

One morning, Father went downstairs to buy milk and bread for breakfast.

At the entrance of the building stood a gatekeeper.

Father greeted him with a friendly **"Good morning, Comrade."**

In return he got an angry look.

In those "happy" days, everybody was a comrade, but not necessarily a friend.

13

When Mother saw Father with a Soviet officer, she was frightened. Father reassured her and explained, "We are being transported to a new location. A truck is waiting downstairs. We must hurry and gather our belongings."

On the way to the train station, Father asked the officer if he could stop at the theater where he worked to pick up his salary. The officer agreed.

When the theater manager saw Father with the officer, he wasn't surprised, because these days it was a common sight.

He said, "We have no money now." But, unlike the other theater manager, he added, "Give me your address where you'll be and we promise to mail you the money."

The officer had no idea where we were being sent, so Father couldn't give him the address.

The manager said, "When you know, send it to us."

The theater manager and the staff were truly sorry to see Father go.

At the Grodno train station, freight cars were waiting. They were packed to capacity with refugees from Poland. The train was guarded by officers of the NKVD, the Soviet secret police. Around midnight, the train left the station.

When we'd come to Belarus from Poland, we'd had few belongings to begin with. This unforeseen change in our destiny resulted in even fewer possessions. What Mother had left in Bialystok was lost forever.

Despite many attempts, we never heard from the gifted young poet Hayim Genelde and his father. Most likely they died in the war and the world lost a great talent, and I certainly lost my first friend.

14

On the train were mostly Jewish refugees, along with a few Poles from regions near the Soviet border. My parents made new friends, among them a couple named Honigman from Warsaw and Rachel, a nurse who had worked in a Jewish hospital in Warsaw. Also on the train were many young kids, some about my age.

In the crowded boxcar was an improvised stove made of a metal barrel. On top was a large pot, where a mushroom and barley stew was cooking. The aroma permeated the car. In my infinite wisdom, I had to make sure that the stove was hot, so I put my hands against the stove. It was quite hot! I got nicely burned hands, which hurt the rest of the trip. I never touched a hot stove again.

When the train arrived at another station, there

came new soldiers. Their officer told us kids, "Say, 'God, give us beans.'" We dutifully repeated. But no beans fell from the sky. Then he said, "Kids, say, 'Soviets, give us candy.'" When we repeated, "Soviets, give us candy," the soldiers gave us candy . . .

This was basic Soviet theology: Don't waste your time asking God for beans; you'll get nothing. Better ask the Soviets—they deliver.

THREE

SETTLEMENT YURA

I

Our journey lasted weeks. The train stopped more often than it traveled. While our train went north, many other trains went west. They were laden with soldiers and supplies going to the western border for the Red Army, as the Soviet Union's army was known. Comrade Stalin's Soviet Union and Hitler's Nazi Germany may have had a nonaggression agreement, but they didn't trust each other.

When we reached our final destination, *Posëlok Yura*, "Settlement Yura," it was the summer of 1940. I was now five years old.

2

Settlement Yura was located all the way north near the White Sea, in the *Arkhangelsk Oblast* (the Archangel region) of the enormous Russian Republic of the Soviet Union.

The settlement was small. There were some wooden barracks and a river nearby, and it was surrounded by endless forests.

We were suspects. Enemies of the Soviet Union. We were now prisoners. However, Settlement Yura had no fences or walls, and no armed guards, or guards of any kind. Guards weren't necessary. The endless Russian forests all around us took care of that. Escape meant certain death. Should you try to escape, you could choose how to die. You could wander in the forests, get lost, never get anywhere, and freeze to death. Or you could be eaten by wild beasts. The choice was yours.

3

The wooden barracks each had a long main room and a few small rooms. We weren't lucky enough to get a small room for ourselves. My parents managed to secure us a corner of the larger room in one of the roughly built wooden buildings. They took one of our two sheets and hung it up to create a bit of privacy for us.

We considered ourselves lucky to have a corner. In those days, a story circulated about a teacher who handed out pictures of Stalin to her students.

The next day, a pupil named Petya brought the picture back.

The teacher asked, "Why didn't you hang the picture at home?"

Little Petya said, "We have no walls. We live in the middle of the room."

We slept on one narrow bed. Mother and Father were at the head of the bed, and I slept at their feet.

Mother had left our warm blanket in Bialystok, but the Honigmans, who had two blankets, kindly let us use one of their own.

4

We were dead tired from the long journey,

but the first night in our new lodgings, no one slept.

The next morning, the settlement director, Ivanov, came and asked, "How was your first night?"

One refugee said, "We couldn't sleep at all."

"Why is that?" asked Ivanov.

"The local bedbugs gave us quite a reception."

"Nichevo!" said Ivanov. "That's nothing! You'll have plenty of time to get used to them, and they'll get used to you."

Later that day, at the assembly in the dining hall, Ivanov gave us his welcome speech: "You were sent here to rebuild your life from scratch. Erase your memories of your life in fascist Poland. Here you will spend the rest of your lives and here you will die."

He pointed at a hill beyond the window. "Over this

hill is the cemetery. That will be your last resting place. Poland you'll never see again. If you work well, you'll eat. If not, you won't eat."

After having thoroughly depressed the assembled newcomers with his welcome speech, Ivanov looked for some comic relief and asked members of the audience to volunteer to sing a song or perform something entertaining.

I don't remember how it happened that I found myself standing on a table, reciting a children's poem in Yiddish that I knew by heart.

Fleegala, meegala, zoomala zoom,

Dos buykhl in gingold aroom oon aroom.

Ein moll guyte dee fleeg in feld oon gefint a tyster gelt.

Loyft zee, loyft zee shnel in mark koyft zeekh ein a samovar.

Tarakanas kimt tsee gyne, kh'vel ikhe gaybn zissen tie.

Ongakoomen tarakanas foon dee vent in karavanas . . .

Toop a taupe, toop a taupe.

Tantsn vantsn off'n cope.

Fly, little fly, zooming zoom,

Her tummy all golden around and around.

One day she walks in a field and finds a wallet with

   money.

She hurries to the market and buys a samovar.

Cockroaches, come, I'll give you sweet tea.

Caravans of cockroaches came out of the walls . . .

Bedbugs are dancing on their heads.

My silly bug story didn't stop there. Suddenly, disaster
strikes. An uninvited spider kidnaps the generous fly,

and the joyful party is about to end in tragedy. But then a valiant mosquito, in the nick of time, kills the spider and rescues the fly. There is great rejoicing. And the mosquito and the fly live happily ever after.

In other words, just the kind of poem that the bewildered audience was dying to hear.

5

Now that we had an address, Father was able
to send a letter to the Gomel theater. To our surprise
and delight, the theater director was true to his promise, and Father received the money due to him for his
work.

It was late summer. There was still ice on the walls
from last winter. This far north, summers were too
short to melt the ice. The well behind the barracks,
where we pulled our water by the bucket each morning, was still partially frozen.

The days were long and the nights short. The sun
went down for a brief time in the middle of the night
and began to shine soon again, which gave us little time
for sleep.

In September it began to snow. It was now approximately one year since we'd left Warsaw, a city almost 2,400 kilometers away.

In Settlement Yura, we had no newspapers, no books, no movies, no radio. I hadn't even heard the word *television*. But we had snow. Lots of snow. And so, for us kids, snow became our entertainment. Temperatures were consistently below freezing. We didn't care.

6

During the day, the sun melted a thin layer of snow. At night the surface froze, forming a thin layer of ice on top of the snow. Like the other kids, I ran on top of the snow's thin ice. Now and then, the thin ice layer gave way, and I fell through the ice into the soft snow underneath. I had to climb up and out of the hole, which was much deeper than I was tall.

Climbing out of the hole was fun. But when snow got into my felt boots and my socks got wet, my toes froze, and that was the end of my entertainment, at least for that day.

7

The men of our settlement, including Father, worked as lumberjacks. They had to walk several kilometers to work. They left early in the morning and returned late in the evening. When my

parents' friend Mr. Honigman came back from work,
I was fascinated by the icicles that hung from his mustache. To me, he looked like Father Winter in person.

8

There were two communal baths, one for men
and one for women. Mother decided she'd do a better
job washing me than Father, so she took me to the
women's bath.

When word got around, the older boys began to pes-
ter me with questions. They wanted to know whether
a certain young redhead was also red below. I didn't
know what they were talking about and I couldn't
have cared less. All I wanted was to get in and get out
of there as fast as possible. The boys kept pestering
me with questions about the redhead.

To get rid of them, I said, "Yes, she is red everywhere."

To tell the truth, all I had seen in the women's bath
was a forest of legs.

But that wasn't enough. They insisted I make a

drawing. Since I was still in my artistic stick-figure
period, I drew a stick figure.

I don't know whether that satisfied their curiosity.
But it worked. Because after that, they never asked me
again. And I never went back to the women's bath, to
make sure they left me alone.

9

The Soviet government established quotas for the amount of work that had to be done. One day, a cart and horse got stuck in the snow. The cart couldn't move despite the poor horse's valiant efforts.

The Russian driver whipped the poor horse and cursed, "You damned counterrevolutionary! You stinking Trotskyist saboteur! Because of you, I won't be able to accomplish my five-year-plan *quota*!" And he kept hitting the horse.

I can still see it in my mind, although I only heard Father telling it to Mother when he returned from work.

10

The soles of Father's shoes had begun to separate from the leather uppers, so while he was working in the woods, snow got into his shoes. As a result, he caught a cold and had a bad fever. The fever wasn't high enough to qualify as an official excuse not to go to work, but since he wasn't feeling well, Mother advised him to rest for a day, so he wouldn't get any sicker.

When Ivanov came to inspect the barracks, like he did every morning, he saw that Father was in bed sleeping. "What do you think you're doing? Do you think you are one of those barons in fascist Poland?"

Father tried to explain that he wasn't drunk or lazy, but that on account of his torn shoes and illness he had stayed in bed . . . to no avail.

The next day, when he returned to his work in the woods, he was told to go back to the settlement immediately. A judge had arrived on horseback, to pass sentence on all those who hadn't shown up for work or had committed other transgressions.

The judge was a young blond woman with braids. She sat at a table next to Ivanov. Father was nervous. He explained that his absence wasn't due to drinking but to a fever because of his torn shoes.

The judge discussed Father's case with Ivanov. Then she said his salary would be cut by fifteen percent for six months, and all special favors he had earned would be suspended.

Later that evening, at the dining hall, Ivanov told Father that he had asked the judge to give Father a light sentence because he hadn't missed work before. But he cautioned him to beware, because the next time his punishment would be ten times more severe.

When Mother heard about the sentence, she regretted having advised Father to take a day off.

11

After what felt like many bitter cold months, some signs of summer reluctantly appeared, and the snows began to melt. We kids didn't wait for the snow to be completely melted to run to the river.

The road to the river was paved with logs. One day in June, as I ran on the wet and slippery logs to catch up with the older boys, I fell. My right arm got caught between two logs, and I broke my elbow.

Father was at work. A messenger was sent to find him and order him to return to the settlement immediately.

Father was terrified that he was being summoned for committing some new work infraction that he didn't know about. But no. It was about his little son, who had broken his arm.

There wasn't an X-ray machine in the settlement.

So Ivanov told Father to take me to the regional hospital. Since train service was only once every twenty-four hours, Father decided we should walk. He reasoned that by walking we'd get to the hospital faster, and my arm would be taken care of sooner.

In order to not get lost, we walked along the railroad tracks. It was an arduous journey. My arm was in a makeshift splint: two pieces of wood held by a bandage in a sling. It was swollen and it hurt.

Despite the pain, I didn't complain. I didn't want to upset Father any more. But I kept asking, "Are we almost there?"

Although Father didn't have the faintest idea where we were, he adopted an air of absolute certainty. "Almost. It's not very far."

I knew he was lying, but his pretense of assurance was comforting. And so we kept walking.

Every now and then, we passed by small wooden huts. The appearance of the poor Russians who lived there conveyed both pride and sadness.

We walked for a whole day.

When we finally got to the government hospital, we were told that they had no X-ray machines either. The Red Army had requisitioned them. The emergency-room doctor said he'd have to set the bone by feel and hope for the best. It was a very painful process, and I prefer not to think about it.

Father went back to Yura, while I stayed in the hospital for one week. Each day, I was given tea and a lump of sugar—such a special treat. Generally, we drank *kipyatok*, which was simply boiled water. I saved the sugar for Mother.

When Father came for me, I left the hospital with a heavy plaster cast on my arm, which I wore for a month. It was itchy and uncomfortable. After it was finally removed by Nurse Rachel, my arm was weak, and moving it felt painful. It took me over another month to regain full mobility.

12

We were able to travel back to Yura by train.
But when we returned from the hospital, we found
Mother lying in bed, near death. She had constant
severe stomach pains. Every day, her condition was
getting worse. Her forehead was on fire from a very
high fever. One of the Jewish refugees from Warsaw
was Dr. Lipshitz. He told Father to put ice compresses
on her forehead and hot-water bottles on her feet,
which were ice cold. He told Rachel, the nurse, to give
Mother injections of camphor every hour to stimulate
her breathing.

When Father went out to get pieces of ice from the
well, Dr. Lipshitz went with him. He told Father, "Your
wife is dying. By dawn tomorrow she may be gone."
Father began to cry.

Mother was loved by everybody. When several

women overheard the doctor's words, they began to weep too.

Father pulled himself together. He was not religious, but now out of desperation he prayed not to lose her at such a young age. Mother was only in her late twenties.

But Mother knew her true state. She told Father in a very weak voice, "We still have two bedsheets from Warsaw. One is torn. The other is not. When I die, you'll wrap me in the torn sheet and save the other, and bury me behind that hill. The sun will shine tomorrow, but not for me. I know you'll be a good father to our little son."

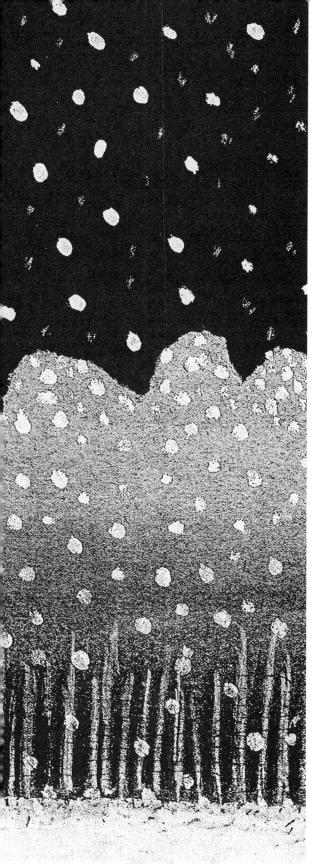

13

Mother survived the night.

Ivanov got a cart and horse to take Mother to the train station, from there to go to the regional hospital, where I had just come from. Dr. Lipshitz went with them.

During the night, there had been a freak snowstorm that covered all the roads.

Fortunately, the horse knew its way and took them to the train station.

The station director provided a stretcher for Mother. The train to the hospital was on the other side of the station.

The Germans
had attacked
the Soviet Union
just days before. The station was packed
with soldiers going to the front.

Long trains, full of soldiers, blocked the way. Father and Dr. Lipshitz decided to
transport Mother underneath the trains instead of going the long way around.

Father crawled on all fours between
the wheels, pulling the stretcher, while
Dr. Lipshitz pushed from behind.

And so they managed to get it to the
other side of the station, where they
took the local train to the hospital.

After this ordeal, the doctor in charge at the hospital said, "Why did you bring her here to die? Couldn't she die where you came from? Why put her through this journey for nothing? We have no medications. All we have is kipyatok."

Hearing these words was a blow.

But Father didn't give up. He kept pleading with her, to no avail.

After Dr. Lipshitz told the doctor his diagnosis, she finally consented to have Mother admitted.

14

Weeks passed after Mother went to the hospital and Father returned to look after me. I didn't know if I would ever see her again. I kept asking him, "How is Mother? When will she be back?"

Finally, one day, she returned from the hospital. She was extremely weak and spent most of the time in bed. Since everyone at the settlement knew and loved her, she got a warm welcome, and there was much rejoicing to have her back.

15

The German invasion of the Soviet Union in the summer of 1941 was a betrayal of the nonaggression pact that had kept the peace between the two countries. Now the Soviet Union joined the Allied forces, including Great Britain and France, who had declared war on Germany.

As a result, the Soviet government's attitude toward us changed dramatically. We who had fled the Nazis were no longer considered anti-Soviet spies or enemies of the state, but merely refugees who had escaped a common enemy.

Eventually, there came from Arkhangelsk, the regional capital, a delegation of NKVD officers, headed by a woman. Judging by the deference of Ivanov and the other NKVD officers, she was a very high-ranking official in the Soviet secret police.

An assembly was called, and she gave a big speech.

She said, "My name is Esther Rachel Greenberg. I come from Moscow on a mission to clarify to you why you're here. You were sent here because we have housing and work. I'm of Jewish origin. I am doing very important and responsible work for the authorities. Only in Soviet Russia could I have reached such a high position. We know the reasons why you came east—because of the Nazi bombs. There were those among us who suspected that you were spies. But now we all have a common goal: to fight the Nazis. Soon your situation will change for the better and you'll be free to travel as you wish. Because of the war, there are some difficulties. But the southeastern part of our country is open to you. You'll be able to travel to all the Central Asian republics."

What Comrade Greenberg didn't say was that now, since the Soviets had joined the Allies to fight the Nazis, it didn't look good to mistreat Western refugees. Hence the radical change in attitude toward us. We were no longer enemies of the Soviet Union.

From then on, our conditions improved, and the attitude of the Russians in charge, starting with Ivanov, was less severe.

16

During work breaks out in the forest, Father and the other refugees often sat around a fire and reminisced about the foods they ate before the war— pastries, chocolate, all kinds of fruits and meats.

One day, when he overheard the refugees' food-filled conversation, the Russian work supervisor said, "At the end of the 1920s was the beginning of the collective farms, the *kolkhozy*, here in the Soviet Union. Peasants were forced to join a *kolkhoz*. Those who refused were deported to Siberia or to other far northern regions. That's why I am here.

"When we arrived, there was absolutely nothing to eat. The hunger was horrendous. Not only here, but all over Russia. We ate whatever we could find. We ate boiled tree bark. We ate shoe leather. People by the thousands died of starvation.

"In a major city in Ukraine, whose name I'm not allowed to divulge, people began mysteriously disappearing. Their bodies were never found. As this was happening, there appeared in the city market delicious buns made of potatoes and filled with meat. They were baked by old babushkas, who sold them. The buns sold like hotcakes, although they were far from it. The babushkas couldn't keep up with the demand. They had no idea what kind of meat it was. The authorities became suspicious. It was soon revealed that the meat suppliers were a criminal gang. They confessed to the murders of those who had disappeared. A revolutionary court condemned them to death. They were hanged in the marketplace where the babushkas had sold the buns. May the earth spit them out of their graves.

"I am ashamed to admit that before I arrived here, I, too, ate one of those buns. I had no idea, until later, what I had eaten. May God forgive me," he finished, and he crossed himself.

17

Sometime after the visit of the NKVD
delegation, Ivanov announced to the parents of small
children that they would be given goats. And so, before
long, we received a goat. Even better, our goat came to
us pregnant. Her name was Vanya. I immediately took

a liking to Vanya. I couldn't get over how a she-goat had a beard.

My acquaintance with Vanya made me a believer that goats had a sense of humor. She was a great jumper. She'd jump on beds and on tables, and leave behind her calling card—a cluster of droppings—as if to say, *Vanya was here.*

In Yura, among the Jewish refugees from Warsaw, was an engineer. He was in his mid-thirties. He was thin, sad-looking, and alone. He had no family—all he had was bad luck. Being delicate, he had great difficulty working as a lumberjack. Whenever something bad happened, it happened to him.

Of all the beds in our barrack, Vanya kept picking his bed upon which to leave her calling card. He didn't get angry, only resigned, as if it was his fate.

Sadly, the man's luck never changed. He didn't survive the war.

18

Vanya spent her summer days roaming around, eating grass. When I called, "Vanya!" she immediately came running, no matter where she was.

One day, she gave birth to twins—a baby he-goat and a baby she-goat. I was very proud of Vanya and showed her off to the other children. Plus, she gave us delicious milk. I will never forget her.

19

There is no spring in the far north. When harsh winters come to an end, suddenly it's summer. Grass has begun to grow under the snow blanket. The melting snows cause floods, and rivers swell up.

Near the rivers were high piles of logs that needed to be sent downstream. Ivanov got an order from his superiors to organize groups of workers to help with the job.

Father was in one of these groups. They were each given two loaves of bread and two smoked fish, and were sent to the train station. When they reached their destination, they were received by the head of a collective farm. The workers were assigned to different houses among the locals.

Father was to stay with an old couple until the logging work was done. At night the old couple lay on top

of a room-sized Russian stove to keep warm. The head
of the collective introduced Father and told them, "I've
brought you a guest to help with the work. Treat him
well. Be generous with kipyatok."

The old couple bowed their heads, hands on their chests, and said, "Welcome," and made the sign of the cross.

Their place was small, modest, and very clean. On the wall there was a picture of Stalin, and, to its right, an icon of a Russian Orthodox saint. To its left was a photo of a young officer with medals for bravery. Father looked at the photo. The old woman wiped a tear and said, "That's my son the war hero, who left and never came back. He was killed by the Germans. But Finnish snipers, too, killed many of our boys."

The old woman boiled water in a pot that had the czarist double-headed eagle insignia on it. She explained, "It's the only thing I have from my parents. They were once rich."

Father took out half a loaf of bread and half a fish and invited them to share it with him.

They refused. But Father saw how they looked at

the food, so he begged them to please join him. They finally agreed. They all finished the meal by drinking kipyatok.

Father asked, "What's the matter with that skinny cow that is dying that I saw outside? Why not heal her or, if that's impossible, butcher her for meat for the people?"

The old man explained, "The cow belongs to the government, not to us."

Father said, "Though the summer is short, there is plenty of great grass to feed the animals."

The old man said, "Last summer was *very* brief. We were shorthanded and didn't have enough time to complete our allotted work. There was no time to gather grass to feed our animals. Worse—now we have food shortages. That's the price we pay for not completing our quotas. To eat the meat is forbidden."

Then he told Father how he'd served in the army

of the czar, the Russian king, in World War I. How he lay in a trench in Poland near Lodz, in the winter of 1914–1915. "In the beginning the czarist army had many victories. We conquered parts of Galicia from the Austrians. We marched on Berlin, confident of victory. But the Germans tricked us. They retreated. Hidden microphones played Russian military songs. They lured us to West Prussia, where there are forests and large swamps. The slaughter of our soldiers was terrible. This defeat was a major contributing factor to the 1917 Bolshevik revolution and the creation of the Soviet regime.

"Being Jewish, Comrade, you know about the drowning of the Egyptian army in the Red Sea, as told in the Bible. Well, we too drowned."

20

When it was time to leave Settlement Yura, we were free to travel south to the Soviet republics in Central Asia, as Esther Rachel Greenberg had promised. There was a very long journey ahead.

Sadly, Vanya and her kids couldn't come with us.

Before our departure, my parents decided to butcher the male kid as food for the road. This upset me so much that I refused to touch the meat.

FOUR
TURKESTAN I

I

Our journey south was long and exhausting.
For more than two months, a small group of us traveled aboard freight trains. Since we had no tickets—either because we couldn't afford them or because they simply weren't available—we were afraid that if we were discovered, we would be arrested.

There were long waits in train stations. We waited for a train for days, sometimes for weeks. A shower was

out of the question. Homeless, we slept on the floor. We forgot what it was like to sleep in a bed.

When I say we slept on the floor, I am not conveying a true picture of what that really meant. While we traveled south, thousands of others were escaping the advancing Nazi armies. At the train station, more times than not, the floor space for stretching out was occupied by multitudes of people waiting for a train, any train. To be able to lie down and stretch out, we sometimes had no choice but to go outside, hoping it wouldn't rain. Lying on the cold, hard ground was far from comfortable, but we also had to sleep with one eye open, like wild animals, because of thieves and other criminals, who were looking for easy victims to rob and, if necessary, kill.

When we reached the city of Turkestan, tired of months of travel under these conditions, it's not surprising that my parents, our friends the Honigmans, and the nurse Rachel decided to stay there.

2

Turkestan was a small city in the Kazakh Republic of the Soviet Union. It was much closer to Iran, Afghanistan, and China than to Warsaw or even to Moscow, the Soviet capital. When we got there, it seemed like a place where life hadn't changed much since the Middle Ages.

The streets had no pavement and no sidewalks. Squat, simple homes were built of earth, straw, and camel dung. Courtyards were ringed with high walls and narrow alleys.

The local Muslims talked about the reign of Tamerlane in the Middle Ages as if it had ended right before the Bolshevik revolution of 1917—as if nothing else of importance had happened in the five hundred years since he ruled.

Both Russians and Kazakhs lived in Turkestan. The city was sliced in two by the railroad. We found a very small, dirt-floored room.

The year was 1942. I was seven years old.

Turkestan was a new world, filled with new customs and even new animals.

The Kazakh women wore long, thick skirts. They'd squat for a few minutes in the middle of the street, their skirts providing privacy, then get up and walk away. I saw the small puddles they left behind. At first we were shocked

by how they dealt with the call of nature. In time we stopped paying attention.

Most Kazakh men carried a razor-sharp, moon-shaped dagger in their belt.

There were many camels and donkeys. I watched how Kazakhs collected their droppings in the street. After drying them in the sun, they used them as fuel for the small clay-lined pits where they baked pitas.

Kazakh women ground wheat by hand using two

large stones. They had no matches. Instead, the men carried a flint, a wick, and a small piece of metal for lighting the droppings on fire in the middle of the fire pits. The women plastered flat, round pieces of dough to the heated walls of the pit. When the pitas were baked, they fell off the wall.

3

Soon after our arrival in Turkestan, Father vanished.

We were frightened. Was he dead? Was he alive? We had no idea. We didn't know where he had gone, or what had happened to him.

"Where is he?" I kept asking Mother. "Will Father ever come back?"

Mother had no answers.

Whatever the reason for Father's disappearance, as far as our lives were concerned, we were abandoned. Now our survival fell on poor Mother's shoulders.

We were in desperate need of food. Mother was still weak from her illness in Yura. But she had to look for work. The only job available was at a nearby construction site, wheeling loads of clay bricks.

It was hard work. When she got home, she was dead tired. She told me that with each step, she felt as if she were sinking into the ground.

While Mother went to work, I stayed home alone. Home was a small room, walls built of the same material as the other houses. Mother was getting paid a meager salary, which wasn't sufficient to buy enough food. As a result, I was constantly hungry and weak.

4

The Nazi armies kept advancing deeper into the Soviet Union. Their aim was to take possession of the oil fields in the Caucasus. The Republic of Chechnya was on the way. We heard that the Chechens had rejoiced at the German advance, viewing them as liberators from Soviet rule, and had sent a white horse as a present to Hitler.

In retaliation, once the Soviets turned back the German invaders, they sent thousands of Chechens into exile. One day, a freight train packed with Chechen exiles arrived in Turkestan.

5

Those were years when we were always
hungry. There weren't even any garbage cans to pick
through for rotten scraps of food to eat. We had nothing. Our situation was dire.

Hunger is hard to describe to someone who has
never experienced it. When my stomach was empty, as
it was most of the time, I felt as if the stomach acids
were eating my insides.

Once, to ease my constant hunger pains, Mother
made me a cutlet out of grass. I enjoyed eating it. But
unlike a cow's multiple stomachs, my one stomach
couldn't tolerate it. As soon as I finished eating, I had
severe diarrhea and had to run to the outhouse.

Going to the bathroom in Turkestan was an adventure. Our outhouse had a low clay wall for privacy. It
had no roof to protect the user from the weather. It was

just a hole in the ground with no toilet seat. When you looked down, you could see thousands of squirming white maggots having a party. No toilet paper: We used stones instead. You can imagine the fun of having to run outside many times with diarrhea and then wipe yourself with stones, which weren't always smooth. Was the grass cutlet worth it?

6

Undernourished and weak, I fell extremely ill. I had a combination of three deadly illnesses. One of them was meningitis.

Mother took me to the hospital. Since the Nazi invasion in 1941, all medication had been sent to the front for the Red Army. At the hospital there was no medication and very little food, either. Even there I was hungry. That I managed to survive is beyond explanation. I don't remember how long I spent in the hospital, but when I finally left, I was so skinny and weak that literally the slightest breeze knocked me down to the ground.

Night after night, I went to bed on an empty stomach, sometimes having eaten only a scrap of bread the entire day, and frequently having eaten nothing at all.

The hunger pains were so severe that I had trouble falling asleep.

My poor, loving mother couldn't feed my body. But she did magnificently feed my mind, which provided a distraction from our situation.

She told me stories. Stories she remembered, sometimes half remembered, to which she would add her own plot twists and endings. I didn't care. Anything would do. Greek myths, fairy tales, stories she had read or heard, films she'd seen. I was grateful for her stories, I loved them. They fired my imagination and inspired my lifelong love of stories, and belief in their importance, with their ability to transport me to faraway places, to experience other people's lives.

Of all the stories Mother told me, my favorite was when I'd ask, "Mother, tell me what we'll eat after the war?"

And she'd say, "We'll have rolls with lots of butter."

"How many rolls could I have?"

And she'd say, "As many as you'd like."

I couldn't believe it.

Before the war, Mother had worked in a bakery owned by her relatives. When I'd ask her to tell me more, she would say, "On a table covered with a beautiful white cloth, there will be a basket of fresh rolls. Their wonderful aroma will permeate the room. The rolls will be golden brown, firm and crunchy on the outside, white, soft, and fluffy on the inside. They'll be buttered with a thick layer of sweet butter. When you take a bite of the roll, it will melt in your mouth."

I'd ask, "What else will we have after the war?"

She'd say, "Oh yes, we'll have thick, sweet hot chocolate."

When I'd ask her to tell me more about it, she would say, "Well, I'll take creamy milk, add cocoa and sugar, and boil it, then whip it and pour it into a glass. There'll be a crown of foam on top. When you take a sip, it'll be sweet as honey and smooth as silk."

I devoured that story. I drank that story. I never tired of hearing it. I'd ask Mother to tell it again and again.

Mother would kindly, patiently, repeat it. I tried hard to imagine what rolls with butter might taste like, but all I could taste was the bitter taste of hunger.

Before the war, in Warsaw, when I was four years old, my parents took me to see Walt Disney's *Snow White*. It was my first film. Now, in Turkestan, if Snow White and the seven dwarfs had decided to come pay me a visit, I wouldn't have been the least bit surprised. But if someone had walked in and brought me a buttered roll, I would have been sure that I was dreaming.

7

In those days, there was no such thing as white bread. If we were lucky, we had a piece of black bread. It contained more water than flour, and as a result it could never be properly baked, so it bore more of a resemblance to modeling clay than to traditional bread.

When we were out of bread—which happened frequently—to distract me, Mother would take a few crumbs she'd saved and knead them into tiny faces. The faces had all kinds of expressions—some were funny, some sad. She was quite good at it.

But then we'd eat them. We couldn't afford to waste crumbs.

8

Drawing was another distraction from the hunger. While Mother slaved at the construction site, I stayed home alone. Drawing helped me pass the time.

Before the war, I drew stick figures marching up and down the margins of Father's newspapers. Father didn't mind. On the contrary, he praised my artistic attempts—provided, of course, that my stick figures stayed obediently in the margins and didn't march on his articles. Why should he have minded my stick figures on his newspapers? Weren't they living proof of his prophecy, that I'd be an artist, coming true?

But those were only memories of long-gone days. Now there were endless, empty days waiting for Mother to return from the construction site, which she did, exhausted and depressed, and I . . . I had to figure out what to do with myself in her absence.

As before, it was drawing, drawing, drawing. But now I had to come up with ways to keep drawing when I had no paper or pencil. For charcoal, I used pieces of half-burned wood. I drew on tree bark, dried leaves, a piece of torn cardboard if I was lucky. Flower petals and crushed green leaves were paint substitutes. I'd squeeze and rub them on top of my drawings. The result was a faint suggestion of color.

Sometimes I scratched drawings with a stick on the ground outside our little room. Other times I'd use a pebble for a head, a small stick for the body, and a small leaf for a hat. Being malnourished, I quickly grew tired, and I'd have to stop.

Then I discovered that drawing with my finger in the air was less tiring. To onlookers, I must have looked like I was insane. No matter: I kept busy.

At other times, I simply looked outside and moved my finger around the contours of neighboring houses and walls, as if touching them from a distance.

That also got tiring. I'd rest in our room. While stretched out on the floor, I'd close my eyes and see in my head imaginary pictures.

Drawing—on a leaf, on the ground, in my imagination—was more than a distraction.

It was my home.

9

Starving and penniless,
we took a walk.

We came upon a field of
tomatoes, peacefully ripening in
the sun.

Mother was desperate.
She was on the edge of
madness.

With great hesitation,
she whispered to me in a
voice so low that she had
to repeat it, **"Uri, go, see if
you can get a tomato."**

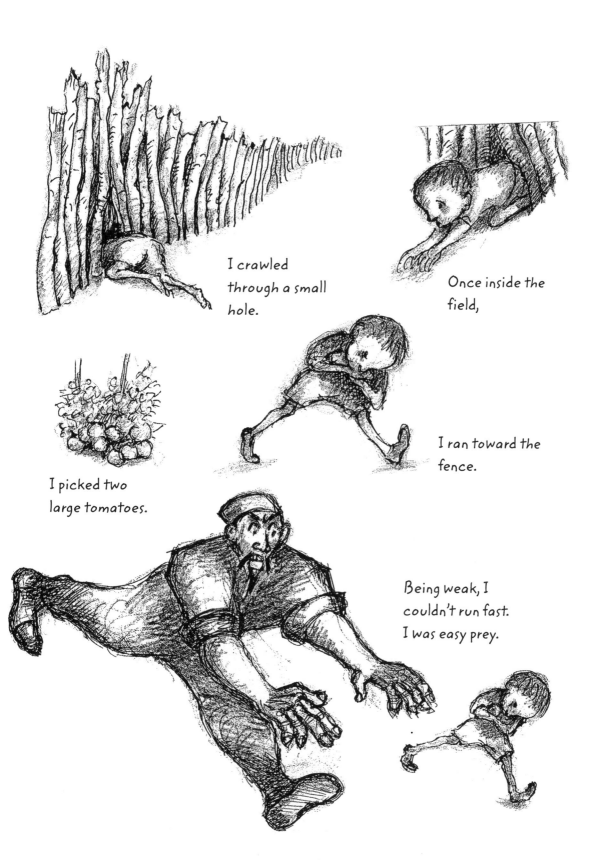

I crawled through a small hole.

Once inside the field,

I picked two large tomatoes.

I ran toward the fence.

Being weak, I couldn't run fast. I was easy prey.

A Kazakh worker caught me.

He grabbed the tomatoes

and hit me in the face so hard that I flew several meters before hitting the ground.

I lay motionless. The Kazakh stood over me for a few seconds, which seemed to me like a very long time.

Finally he walked away. I crawled out of the field, my face on fire. I dragged myself toward Mother.

Her face was ashen.

"Dear God," she said, half talking to herself, "what have I done? How could I have risked my little boy's life for a tomato? I'll never, ever do something like that again. I'd rather we die."

We walked home in silence.

Could our miserable lives sink any lower?

This is one of my most painful memories.

10

Mother had lost all hope that we'd ever see
Father again. She decided we should leave the city and
go to a nearby kolkhoz. She thought that perhaps on
the collective farm we'd have a better chance of surviving.

At the kolkhoz, Mother worked in the fields har-
vesting sugar beets, the main crop. Having no friends
my age, I sat and watched an elderly Russian basket weaver work. I spent hours watching him create
baskets from long, thin tree branches. Next to him
was a large metal basin filled with water, in which he
soaked the branches to increase their flexibility.

Our stay on the kolkhoz didn't last very long. I fell
ill once more, and Mother decided to take me to the
hospital in Turkestan. Before our departure, the kindly

basket weaver, to make me feel better, promised that when I returned from the hospital, he'd teach me basket weaving.

I had a high fever. I was dizzy. I had trouble walking. My poor mother had to carry me. We took a narrow, sandy path back to Turkestan. When we were almost a kilometer out of the kolkhoz, Mother remembered that she had forgotten her small saw and that she had to go back and get it. In order not to have to carry me back and forth, she told me to sit down and wait for her there, and she left in a hurry.

Where "there" was, was the Kazakh steppe. As far as the eye could see were flat plains, without a single tree, and only occasional low, dry shrubs. I sat by the narrow path, on slightly elevated ground.

I sat there, sick and alone, not a single soul in sight. Time dragged by slowly. The day was growing dim. I waited.

At some point, I heard a rooster crowing. The faint sound came from far away. And Mother was still not back. I waited.

It was almost dark when, at long last, Mother returned. Her face was flushed and dripping with sweat. She carried her small saw.

She told me that she had lost her way and had had trouble finding the path where she had left me. She kept calling me, and I, in my feverish state, had thought it was a rooster crowing.

As it turned out, getting lost was the least of what had happened to her. When she was at the edge of the kolkhoz, just leaving to come back to me, a group of Kazakh men surrounded her, blocking her way. When one of them came forward, about to grab her, she swung her saw across his face with lightning speed, cutting his cheek, drawing blood. They were stunned. Now, respectfully, they let her pass. She walked away at a rapid pace, almost running, for fear they'd change their minds. She disappeared into the darkness.

My brave mother! Although she was a sweet, gentle soul, in times of crisis she rose to the occasion and showed unexpected courage.

She told me later that when the Kazakhs were attempting to take advantage of her, what flashed through her mind was, *I'm on my own. No one will help me. My little sick boy is waiting. If I don't* return, *he'll die.*

We never went back to the kolkhoz. I never became a basket weaver.

When I think about myself alone, defenseless, in the Kazakh steppe, where wild beasts roamed, I imagine my poor mother finding only a pile of bones on her return, where I used to be. I remember and I shudder.

Back in Turkestan, I stayed once more in the hospital. Mother returned to work at the construction site. We moved back into our old room.

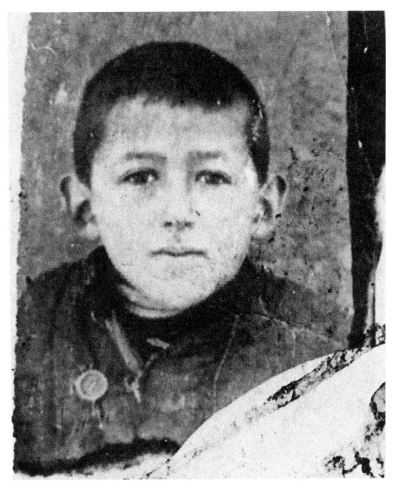

Uri, seven and a half or eight years old, in Turkestan

11

One day, I used the clay walls of our room as a drawing surface. I had set out to draw my usual stick figures. I got very excited when I noticed that my figures were acquiring a faint resemblance to people.

But when Mother came home from work and saw my wall decorations, she wasn't amused. She paid little attention to my progress. She was angry. "Uri, what have you done? Would you like our landlady to throw us out into the street?" Mother was right. That possibility hadn't crossed my mind while I was busy drawing.

There was no arguing. That very night I was busy cleaning the wall. Luckily, charcoal erases easily, and we didn't end up on the street. But my proud figures were gone.

12

In the summer, our small room became stifling hot and dangerous. Dangerous, because poisonous tarantulas called *falanga* came out of the cracks in the walls. So we slept outdoors to escape the tarantulas and the heat. The nights outside were cooler, but they had their own hazards. Sometimes it rained and we had to move back inside.

One evening I was sitting outside, near our sleeping spot, my right hand on the ground. It felt like a needle had entered my finger and kept moving up my arm. The pain kept getting worse. It was the poisonous bite of a scorpion. I was sick for three days.

I was also the victim of blood-sucking lice, which were our constant companions of misery. No matter how hard we tried, we couldn't get rid of them.

The Kazakhs had a simple way of dealing with lice. They would kill a louse by crushing it with a thumbnail against one of their front teeth, then suck the louse's blood. When asked, "How can you do that?" the answer was, "It's my blood. I'm just taking back what was taken from me."

FIVE
TURKESTAN II

I

One day, Father reappeared.

He had been gone for months.

He came back with a large onion as a peace offering.

Mother was furious. I've no idea what they talked about in their long, heated discussions. Did he tell her why and where he went? Did he tell her what happened? I don't know. I do know that Mother was quite angry, and so was I.

It took a long time for us to forgive him. We considered it a betrayal. Even after the forgiveness, a blot remains forever, lessening with time but never totally forgotten. To this day, this incident remains a mystery to me. I still kick myself that I failed to ask him about it. Now that he is no longer alive, I'll never know the truth.

Father was impulsive. I suspect that perhaps he made an attempt to join the Polish army being formed in Iran after he heard about it from Mr. Honigman, who decided to join and was accepted. Father may have decided on the spur of the moment to join as well, and was rejected.

He never left us again.

Father's friend Mr. Honigman, in his Polish army uniform, after the war

2

The construction work was beyond Mother's strength. Father's return, finally, enabled her to quit her job. Father now went to work at the construction site where she had worked. Like her, he got the same very meager salary, which was only enough for the three of us to not die of hunger, not enough to buy us food on the illegal black market to supplement our diet.

All day long I crowed like a rooster, "I am hungry! I am hungry!"

My parents decided to take me to a children's home,

hoping I'd be better fed there.

3

In the morning at the children's home in
Turkestan, they gave us our food for the entire day: a
thick wedge of black bread. The bread was soggy, like
a sponge. If you squeezed it, water would drip out.

When I first arrived, I ate part of my bread and
saved the rest for later. But there was no later. An older,
stronger kid grabbed the bread from my hand. He ate
my bread, and I was too weak to fight him. I learned
my lesson. From then on, I ate my entire piece of bread
fast, like all the other kids.

When the kids woke up in the mornings, most of
them couldn't open their eyes. Their eyes were glued
shut with dry pus from trachoma. I was among the few
who didn't have it.

One day, I was standing around in the yard, and
an older Russian boy who had the infection snuck up

behind me, took some pus from his eyes, and smeared it on mine. He said, "Now you'll be like the rest of us." Equality was a big virtue in the communist Soviet Union, provided you overlooked that some were more equal than others. And so I became an "equal." I got trachoma.

That was the last straw. I had had enough.

When my parents came to visit, I told them, "I'd rather starve at home than be here another day." And so my parents took me home.

4

One day, a couple moved in with us: a writer and his wife from Warsaw.

My parents and the new couple talked for hours late into the night. I don't know what they discussed; I wasn't really interested. All I wanted was the break from hunger pains that sleep could temporarily provide. I'd bury my head under the blanket and go to sleep while the grown-ups kept talking. Perhaps that was their way of forgetting about hunger and the war.

The philosopher Descartes said, "I think, therefore I am." I was no philosopher, but I could have said then, "I'm *hungry*, therefore I am." I don't know about Monsieur Descartes, but I badly wanted a temporary break from my "I am."

5

I was enrolled in first grade at the Turkestan
Russian School. Unlike the small room we lived in, the
school was a large brick building. Our classroom had
a blackboard and wooden desks. Our teacher was a
young Russian woman.

On the first day at my new school, teachers inspected
whether we wore red stars, to show off our patriotism
for the Soviet Union. Those who didn't have one were
sent home.

Most kids had shiny metal stars. I had none. I was
sent home.

Father found a small piece of cardboard, cut it in the
shape of a star, and painted it red. And I was allowed
back in the classroom.

There I learned to read and write Russian. I

befriended some other children of refugees. I was an *otlichnik*—a student who got excellent grades. I also excelled in art, so the teachers and the students started calling me *khudozhnik*, artist.

6

One day, one of many such days when we had barely eaten, Father went to the market with very little money in his pocket to buy food for supper.

He left late in the afternoon. Evening was fast approaching, and he hadn't yet returned. "Did he disappear again?" I worried.

He did return, however, when it was dark. He came back with a long paper roll under his arm.

"What's that?" I wondered.

"What did you get?" Mother asked.

"I bought a beautiful map," he said.

"A map! What about food?"

"I spent hours searching for something to eat for the little money we had. The map was the only thing we could afford."

"Then tonight we'll have the map for dinner," Mother concluded bitterly.

I was angry. My guts were on fire. They were screaming, *I'm hungry! I want food, not a map!*

It was another night that I went to bed on an empty stomach. Meanwhile, the couple we lived with ate their meager supper. Oh! How loudly the husband chewed. He chewed his small crust of bread with such enthusiasm, as if it were the most delicious morsel in the world. I covered my head with my blanket so I would not hear him smacking his lips with such noisy delight.

The next day, Father hung up the map. It showed the Soviet Union and surrounding countries in Europe and Asia and parts of Africa. Our drab room was suddenly flooded with color. As much as I hated to admit it, the map made a big impact on my life.

When I could salvage anything on which to draw, I began to copy sections of the map. I initiated map games with my friends as well. I'd pick a place on the

A section of Father's map I drew at age ten

map and ask one of them to locate it, and then I'd ask them to do the same with me. As a result, I could visualize traveling across countries, continents, and oceans.

Looking at the map, I savored the strange-sounding names. They made such an impression on me that years later I invented little rhymes from the exotic sounds:

Fukuoka Takaoka Omsk,
Fukuyama Nagayama Tomsk,
Okazaki Miyazaki Pinsk,
Lithuania Transylvania Minsk!

I spent hours in front of that map, dreaming of all kinds of places, fantasizing about being there and going on adventures. The piece of mushy bread that Father might have bought with the money would have long ago been eaten and forgotten, but not that map, which I still remember after so many years.

7

Now, a word about my parents.

Father was an optimist. He believed that things would work out for the best. Mother was a pessimist. She had little confidence in the future. Mother had become an orphan at age nine. She'd then gone to live with relatives, who treated her like a servant.

Being an optimist must be better for one's health, since Father seldom got sick. Whereas Mother, the pessimist, was frequently ill.

My parents cared deeply for each other. Yes, I know, Father's disappearance can hardly qualify as an act of deep caring. But he came back. Call it "caring interrupted," because they continued to care for each other for the rest of their lives, and Father never disappeared again.

After all, they were human. And since they were

human, they weren't always of the same opinion, and since they didn't always agree with each other, their disagreements sometimes reached very vocal heights. Father was impulsive and had a bit of a temper. So their arguments, though infrequent, got very loud.

At such times, loud or not, infrequent or not, their disagreements were very upsetting to me. I'd go to them and announce loudly, "I'll never get married!"

Then Father would say, "Oh no, Urechku"—little Uri—"don't say such a thing. Marriage is very good." I wasn't so sure. And Mother would declare, "Uri, dear, bachelors are enemies of society."

I certainly didn't wish to be an enemy of society. Plus, I still had plenty of time to make up my mind about marriage. I wasn't sure what I'd think when I grew up.

There was only one thing I was quite sure of right then—I was hungry.

8

Some refugees sold their meager possessions
in order to buy food.

A fellow refugee from Warsaw told us that he sold his porcelain chamber pot to a Kazakh. He recounted, "Sometime later, I saw the man, who greeted me like an old acquaintance. We talked. One thing led to another, and he invited me for dinner. I was starving and had nothing left to sell, so I gladly accepted his invitation.

"We sat on a carpet on the floor, as is the custom. While we waited for the food to be served, I told my host about life in Poland. The aroma of cooking filled the room. I looked forward to the meal. I could hardly wait to eat.

"Finally a delicious-smelling rice pilaf with lamb was brought out on a large flat platter. As you know, hospitality is very important in the Muslim tradition.

Since I was the honored guest, my food came out in a special pot. When I saw what was in front of me, despite my hunger, I lost my appetite.

"The pilaf was served in none other than my old familiar porcelain chamber pot. I couldn't insult my hosts, who'd had the best intentions and were innocent of the pot's past history. The same couldn't be said of me. I had to pretend to enjoy the food. I struggled to forget what the pot had been used for back in Poland. I swallowed each bite with great difficulty. Needless to say, as delicious as the pilaf was, and as hungry as I was, I didn't enjoy the meal.

"The moral of the story," he concluded, "is that you can't always foresee the consequences of your actions."

One day, I saw a Kazakh promenading in a pair of pajamas as if he were wearing an elegant evening suit. He must have bought the pajamas from a refugee.

9

Father eventually quit his job at the construc-tion site. There was no point working for starvation wages. Instead, my parents tried various ventures, such as making soap to sell at the town's marketplace. The results were far from spectacular, and we remained hungry.

One day, Father decided to build a loom to make fabric. He remembered seeing a loom years before in Poland, and he did it from memory. He purchased wood and began to build in our small room. The construction lasted over a month. As the loom grew, our living space shrank. We lived in the margins around the loom. Soon we had to slide sideways along the walls to get from one side of the room to the other. The couple who shared our room were very understanding and patient.

After much ado, the loom was ready for action.

Father activated the loom. We watched with anticipation. Finally it produced a small piece of fabric about three by five inches. It soon became quite clear that Father's cleverness and skill in building the loom had no practical use. Father had many talents. But one talent he sorely lacked was how to make money, and we remained hungry.

10

No one in Turkestan had electricity except government institutions. For lighting we used kerosene lamps. These lamps required a glass chimney, which often broke. Replacements were unavailable. To solve this problem, Father made our own glass chimneys from bottles.

He tied the bottom of the bottle with a string dipped in kerosene, then lit the string on fire. After the fire had run its course, he hit the bottom of the bottle gently against a stone until it fell off. I polished the rough edges on a stone until the glass was ready to be used. But when the lamp chimney cracked, as it often did, we had to make another one.

II

A year or more had passed since we had arrived. The war continued to rage. There were severe shortages of everything, especially of food. To survive, everybody bent the law, in spite of the risk of imprisonment for years in a Siberian gulag, a forced labor prison far away in the wilderness.

Father wasn't a smoker. But to habitual smokers, a cigarette meant more than bread.

The city of Dzhambul, located between Alma-Ata and Tashkent in the Kazakh Republic of the Soviet Union, grew the finest tobacco. After discussing it with Mother, Father decided to risk going to Dzhambul to buy tobacco and sell it in Turkestan at a profit. Since he had no money, he partnered with Mr. Honigman, who advanced him the money.

When Father finally returned, he told us about his eventful trip.

"When I got to the train station, even though it was very early, there were already multitudes of people waiting for the train. And there was a shortage of tickets. When the train to Dzhambul finally came, the only way to get on was to give the conductor a couple of rubles to look the other way. The train was packed. Like many other passengers without tickets, I stood in the corridor for hours, for the entire ride.

"When I got to Dzhambul, I went straight to the central marketplace and bought tobacco without difficulty. I rushed back to the train station to get home as soon as possible. When I got to the station, military inspectors were searching for and arresting draft dodgers.

"You can imagine how tense I felt when my turn came to be inspected. I showed my papers that I was a Polish citizen, and that I wasn't subject to serve in the

Red Army. It was a relief. But when they demanded to inspect my backpack, they of course found my package of tobacco, so I was detained for questioning.

"After waiting once more, when my turn came to be questioned, they asked me why I had so much tobacco. I said I was a big smoker, and that the tobacco was for my own personal use, and they let me go.

"At the train station, there was a small kiosk selling patriotic brochures. I got a great idea. I bought a brochure with a picture of Lenin on its cover. After all, as a leader of the Bolshevik revolution, Lenin is the patron saint of Soviet Russia.

"When I got on the train for the ride back to Turkestan, on which again I had to stand for hours all the way, I made sure Lenin's face on the brochure was visible.

"There were inspectors on the train checking packages. Some packages were being confiscated, and there were some people being arrested. Once more I was quite tense. When the inspectors saw my brochure

with Lenin's picture, out of respect they didn't bother to examine my backpack. I congratulated myself for buying the brochure. It was a smart move.

"Lenin saved me from arrest. I could breathe easier. And so, despite the roadblocks and risks, I managed to get back to Turkestan without getting arrested and the tobacco confiscated."

12

Father made it back to Turkestan. But his adventure was far from over.

"It was now late afternoon. I hadn't eaten all day. After the long ride, and the tension, I felt hungry and tired. I stopped at the restaurant at the train station. I had soup and a piece of bread. Then I headed home. When I got there, to my surprise, the landlady told me that you had moved and she gave me a note

with your new address, which was all the way across town. I rushed to that neighborhood, with which I was totally unfamiliar, never having been there. I assumed a cheaper room had suddenly come up and you had to move quickly before somebody else took it.

"I walked through the narrow alleys with their

high walls of private courtyards, searching for the new address. It was getting dark, making the search more difficult.

"As I walked in a very narrow alley, a powerful hand grabbed my backpack and someone shouted in Russian, 'Stop! Tobacco speculator!' With his other hand the man grabbed my arm and yelled, 'Come to the police!'

"I suspected that the man's accent wasn't Russian but Polish, and that he might be a fellow refugee, posing as a Russian. As it turned out, he too suspected that I wasn't Russian.

"Now Lenin couldn't come to my aid. I was on my own. After all I'd gone through, I wasn't going to surrender my tobacco, obtained with so much difficulty. I resisted as best as I could. We began to wrestle. I could see that my opponent was a strong man and certainly not as tired as I was. Suddenly, the thief began to speak Yiddish with a Warsaw accent. He said to me, 'I see you're no sucker. You might have a wife, and perhaps children. My wife and I—we too need to make a living, not only you, the speculator. Yes, I am a thief. I'm only doing my job. A thief too has a heart. I'll tell you what I'll do for you, since you are a fellow countryman—we'll divide the tobacco fifty-fifty.'

"The alleys were deserted. Nobody was around. The thief was a strong man. I was quite tired. I didn't see how I could have the upper hand. Even if I got rid of him, there might be other robbers and cutthroats. I decided it might be wiser to agree to his 'generous' offer. So I asked him, 'Where shall we do this transaction, here in the alley?'

"He said, 'I propose we go to my place. It is not far from here. I give you my thief's word of honor that no harm will come to you. My name is King—an honorable name. I'm known in Turkestan. I settle disputes between thieves. You could even spend the night at my place.'

"I felt that I had little choice. How was I going to find the new address in the dark? So I said, 'I accept your offer.'

"King's place wasn't far. It was lit by a kerosene lamp. When we entered his room, I smelled the aroma of fried pancakes.

"King said to his wife, 'Bronia, I brought an unexpected guest. A refugee like us. I met him on the street. We did business. He agreed to give up half of his tobacco, and in return he'll spend the night here.'

"Bronia, who was also from Warsaw, said, 'Feel at home. You've nothing to fear here. My husband is a thief with a conscience and a golden heart.'

"'Bronia, dear,' said King, 'our guest is hungry and so am I. Let's have your delicious pancakes.'

"King took out a bottle of vodka, poured three glasses, and asked me, 'Where are you from?'

"I said, 'Warsaw.'

"King said, 'We must drink a toast to our city.' I didn't like having a toast with my robber, so I said, 'I can't drink, I have a sore throat, but I'll eat the pancakes.'

"As I ate, I thought, *Only thieves could afford such delicious pancakes.*

"King and Bronia emptied their vodka in one gulp. After the meal, King said, 'Now let's divide the tobacco.'

"After this was done, Bronia prepared a place for me to sleep. King asked me, 'What are you going to do with your share? Sell it at the marketplace? Sell it to me. I'll pay you a fair-market price.'

"I thought perhaps there might be inspections at the market, and the police might confiscate the rest of my tobacco. So I agreed to sell my share.

"King gave me the money and said, 'In my place you've nothing to worry about. You're safe here. Outside, that's another matter.'

"I had a fitful night. I woke up periodically, and I made sure my money was still there. I couldn't wait for morning.

"When morning finally came, King said, 'Nothing missing? Do you have all your money?'

"I nodded yes.

"Bronia said, 'Have a glass of tea before you leave.' I showed her the note with the new address. 'Do you know where this is?'

"When she saw the name of the landlady, she grew pale and nearly fainted. She finally said, 'The name of the landlady is Yudayat—she is our landlady here. A couple and a woman with a small boy, whose name is Uri, from Warsaw, moved in next door. Is she your wife? Are we next-door neighbors?'

"Bronia showed me your door. I couldn't forgive myself. Had I known that only a thin wall separated me from you, I wouldn't have surrendered my tobacco to my robber."

When my parents saw them in the courtyard, which was bound to happen, since they lived next door, King and Bronia were embarrassed.

King said, "I had no idea that I robbed a neighbor. But let bygones be bygones. That's the past. I hope we can be friends in the future."

My parents had no such desire. They never became friends.

13

Father's impractical enterprises, such as building a loom, were a failure. His tobacco venture had been no great success either. Plus, speculation was against the law in the Soviet Union; it could have landed him in a Siberian gulag, and we would have never seen him again.

Father had to get a legitimate job. Luckily, he found work in a shoe factory. Father was a fast learner. He was trained how to make new shoes and boots as well as how to repair old ones. Although the salary wasn't much better than at the construction site, the job wasn't as exhausting, he learned new skills, and he didn't have to work in the burning hot sun.

14

Once again, Mother fell ill. Father took her to the hospital. During her stay there, which seemed to me very long, patients got once a day a glass of real tea and a special treat, a luxury in those days: a small lump of sugar. Instead of having it with her tea, Mother saved it.

Another woman's bed was next to hers. She had a Russian book with illustrations. After lengthy negotiations, Mother bartered her sugar for the book. When she finally came home, she gave me the book, making me the happiest kid alive. It was my very first book of my very own. The book was a Russian translation of Charles de Coster's *Tyl Ulenspiegel* with woodcut illustrations by Frans Masereel.

Reading the book—wait, reading? I didn't read the book; I devoured it! When I came to the end, I wished it would go on and on. I was hungry for more. So I extended it in my mind. Eyes shut, I viewed it like my private film, over and over again.

Tyl Ulenspiegel is the story of Tyl, a prankster and the hero of the land of Flanders, and of his friend Lamme Goedzak. It takes place in the sixteenth century, when Tyl's land is under the oppressive rule of Spain. Tyl is seeking to avenge his father's unjust death by the Spanish Inquisition. Lamme is searching for his wife, who has left him.

Tyl is walking on the road, followed by a small dog, when he first encounters Lamme Goedzak. Lamme is sitting by the side of the road, a basket of sausages and a bottle of wine next to him. He is stuffing his mouth with meat and sipping wine, all the while with gloomy tears running down his fat cheeks. As I read this scene over and over, my mouth watered, and I felt as if I were partaking in his feast.

*Tyl Ulenspiegel meets Lamme, which I drew at age eleven,
from an unforgettable memory of my first book*

15

We lived hand to mouth week after week, month after month. Much time passed in this way. Two years? Three? It's hard to remember.

One day, a man with a horse and buggy came to our neighborhood, where most Jewish refugees lived. A horse and buggy was quite rare in Turkestan. A man who had such means of private transportation must be a very important man, no doubt the director of a Soviet government factory or institution.

He announced that he was looking for an artist sign painter and that he needed him urgently. When Mother heard this, she went to him and said, "Comrade Director, you must be looking for my husband. He is a talented sign painter from Warsaw." She told the man to wait and went to tell Father, who was home from work, that an important man was looking for him.

When Father came, the man invited him to sit next to him on the buggy—a great honor. The onlookers looked at Father with envy.

Before they left town, he said to Father, "I'm the director of the Vintorg, a store of military goods. I want to make sure that you won't go hungry. We'll stop first at the Vintorg." When he came back from the store, he gave Father a well-baked, beautiful loaf of bread wrapped in a newspaper. Father was overjoyed in equal measure for the bread and for the newspaper. He was an avid reader of the press, and newspapers were hard to come by.

Then they rode out of town. On the way, the director switched from Russian to Yiddish. He said to Father, "My name is Boris Mirkin. I'm from Leningrad. I'm in Turkestan to manage the Vintorg."

They stopped near a mosque half in ruins. Nearby was a cemetery of Bukharan Jews. The cemetery was in a state of neglect: The caretakers had been drafted into the Red Army. The area was deserted; no one was around, except Boris Mirkin and Father.

Half of the fence was in disrepair. The gate was broken. The cemetery had a lonely, sad-looking tree. Mirkin tied his horse to the tree and brought a pail of fresh water and food for the horse. It was obvious he treated his horse kindly.

Mirkin then led Father to a tombstone and said, "My dear father, may his memory be blessed, lies here. He died right after our arrival in Turkestan. When the war ends, we'll be returning to Leningrad, and my dear father will be left alone. Who will come then to say the prayer for the dead for him? Sorry, I have forgotten what it is called."

Father said, "You must mean the Kaddish."

"*Da, da*—yes, yes, Friend Artist," said Mirkin. From

time to time he looked around to make sure they were alone, because religion was banned in the Soviet Union. But no one was there, except Mirkin, Father, and the horse, eating grass peacefully.

Father recited the prayer for the dead in Aramaic, and Mirkin repeated it after him, with tears in his eyes, deeply moved. Father had studied in a religious school and knew the Hebrew and Aramaic prayers and scriptures well.

Mirkin explained to Father that he had commissioned the tombstone from a Bukharan Jew—from the city of Bukhara 130 kilometers to the west—who was then drafted into the army and didn't have a chance to begin to fill in the Hebrew letters with paint or decorate the tombstone. Mirkin asked Father to please find the right paints to fill in the faded, half-erased Hebrew letters and to decorate the tombstone.

Father promised to look for the paints. And they rode back from the cemetery like old friends.

16

Soon thereafter, Father heard of a Russian widow who was selling her deceased husband's paints and brushes. The woman's husband had been a painter of religious icons and had secretly sold them to devout Russians, who would hang a religious icon next to a picture of Lenin or Stalin.

Father bought the oil paints and brushes as well as turpentine from the widow. Equipped with these supplies, he was able to keep his promise to Mirkin. He painted the Hebrew letters and decorated the tombstone beautifully. When he was done, Mirkin's father's tombstone stood proudly next to forgotten, half-broken tombstones with impossible-to-read names. Father had at long last found an opportunity to express some of his talents. Mirkin was delighted with the results and grateful for all that Father had done.

17

In those days, good connections meant every-thing. Father didn't have any connections. Boris Mirkin did. He put in a good word to the right people, and Father was given a kiosk for shoe repair. Few were so lucky to land such an opportunity—to be his own boss and earn a living.

Father had learned all the necessary skills working in the shoe factory. Since everything was in short supply, Father found ingenious ways to compensate. For example, instead of nails, he used handmade staples and rabbitskin glue to attach the upper part of the shoe to the sole.

The kiosk was very modest. It was a wooden crate standing upright. But it was well located at the market-place, which was in the center of town. The loudspeak-ers that announced the news from the government

radio station were within earshot of the kiosk. While
Father worked, he listened all day to the news reports.
At the end of the day, fellow refugees gathered around
the kiosk to hear from Father about the progress of the
war.

Heated discussions followed. Although none of the refugees had ever served a single day in the military, as if by magic every one of them had become an instant general. They argued about the best strategy. Only they knew how to quicken the road to victory. Those who knew the least talked the most. They went as far as to offer up detailed advice for Marshal Zhukov, the brilliant commander in chief of the Red Army. Marshal Zhukov, of course, paid no attention to the self-appointed generals, being thousands of kilometers away, busy giving the German forces a hard time.

After vigorous back-and-forth arguments, the refugees were exhausted. They were also very pleased with themselves, as if they had won a major victory.

18

After Father got the kiosk, our situation
improved dramatically. Although we never got rich, we
no longer starved, and I no longer went to bed on an
empty stomach.

I visited Father frequently after school. I'd sit by the
side of the kiosk on a small stool
normally reserved for his cus-
tomers. Spending time at the
marketplace, I got to see much
of Turkestan's life, because at
one point or another, for one
reason or another, everyone
ended up making an appear-
ance there, including Mother. She came by from time
to time to talk to Father and see how he was doing.

When Father could afford it, he would give me a

ruble. As the lucky owner of my own ruble, I felt rich, and I might buy a couple of pencils. I could splurge on a secondhand wooden pencil box, a major acquisition. Or maybe I might treat myself to a piece of sweet sun-dried melon, which tasted like candy.

19

The Chechen refugees in Turkestan either couldn't or wouldn't adapt to life in exile. I never understood why, only that we saw them dying one by one from illness and hunger.

Eventually, there was only a lone Chechen survivor left. He was very sick. He had dysentery and looked like a living corpse. He was weak.

With his remaining strength, he would grab a pita from a Kazakh woman vendor and run. While running, he would stuff the pita in his mouth, trying to swallow as much as possible, since when he was caught, which he always was, the Kazakhs chasing him couldn't take from him what he'd already swallowed. But when he was caught, they beat him mercilessly. It was horrifying to see.

The same scene repeated itself day after day.

And then he died.

20

As I sat next to Father's kiosk, I saw young
Russian hooligans who had a more effective way of
stealing food at the marketplace than the lone Chechen.

For example, they would walk in a group by a vendor of apples. Several of them would distract the vendor, while one, carrying a long, stiff wire, bent at the
end into a sharp-pointed hook, would snag an apple
from a distance without the vendor knowing.

2 1

In addition to his shoe-repair work, Father was recommended by Mirkin to other store directors who needed banners.

One day, the train-station director commissioned Father to write banners praising the victories of the Red Army, and banners in praise of Marshal Stalin.

After he delivered the banners, Father went to the train station to get paid. When he got there, he saw the director, with lowered head, being escorted away in handcuffs by two NKVD officers. Had he committed a crime against the Soviet state? Had he been falsely accused? Who knows? All we knew was that Father didn't get paid for his work this time. But he did make a little money now and then from similar jobs.

22

As time passed, I made lots of friends. We kids lived in our own world.

There were about ten of us, all refugees. Mostly boys of eight and nine, and a couple of slightly younger girls. Our lives centered around one another's courtyards.

When we were in our courtyards, we were protected by the high, rough clay walls that surrounded them. Once outside in the streets or in the narrow alleys, it was a war zone. There were gangs of young Russian troublemakers roaming around. An encounter with them meant we would be robbed of whatever we carried. And, as an extra bonus, they would beat us up.

Then there were the older Kazakh kids, who considered it their mission in life to give us refugees a hard time. They'd chase us, and they weren't above beating us up as well and "liberating" us from our possessions.

To avoid such encounters, we took long, circuitous routes to get to our destinations. Although such maneuvers lessened the chance for encounters of the unfriendly kind, they were not foolproof.

Another strategy to meet friends was to avoid the streets altogether and climb over walls to go from one courtyard to another. There was, however, a price to pay—scraped knees, ripped pants, loss of essential buttons on which the integrity of the pants depended, or some other little surprise.

One such little surprise came when I was climbing a wall to meet my friends. I jumped down on the other side, into the courtyard of some new neighbors, and a large, fierce dog was waiting, as if he had been expecting me. He growled disapprovingly, as if to say *Watch out, kid, you're in trouble.*

I'd heard that if you lie down, a dog won't attack. Immediately, I threw myself on the ground and didn't move. The dog seemed surprised. He came over and

sniffed my face. Then he sat down next to me, close enough to offer me a generous dose of his foul breath. He sat and watched me. When I made the slightest movement, he growled a warning. I lay there motionless for what seemed a very long time—especially when a fly landed on my face and I couldn't wave it off with my hand. At long last, the dog got bored with me and decided to attend to more interesting business.

This same routine happened a few more times. Eventually, the dog and I became old acquaintances, and when he saw me, I got a friendly tail wagging instead of growls and a dental display.

23

Around that time, my friends and I were in
the process of digging a secret underground hideout in
a friend's courtyard. The plan for our hideout was to
first dig a hole downward, and then dig a connecting
horizontal tunnel.

Digging wasn't easy. The summer heat and the

hard ground made sure of that.
We had to take periodic breaks.
While we rested, one of our
friends whose father worked in
a bakery would pass out some
wheat grains. This was an occasion for improvised chewing
gum.

We'd each put a couple of

grains in our mouths and begin to chew, grinding the wheat grains with our teeth, being careful not to swallow them. We chewed patiently, until we ended up with a rubberlike, chewable substance. Now began some energetic chewing, which lasted until our jaws got tired and we returned to digging.

One day, when we had begun to dig horizontally inside the hole, one of our friends came running in a panic. He jumped into the hole and cowered in the corner.

He told us what had happened. As he was coming over to join us, a Kazakh kid found him on the street and wouldn't let him pass. No matter how hard our friend tried to avoid a confrontation, he finally lost his patience. He got angry, and after a scuffle he kicked the kid in the groin.

His attacker began screaming at the top of his lungs. To his own and our friend's horror, he was bleeding profusely from the spot where he had been kicked.

Apparently, the kid was thirteen and had recently been circumcised, according to local custom, and wasn't fully healed.

When our friend saw what he had done, he ran for his life.

We rushed to gather anything we could find to camouflage the hole, to protect him from being caught. Had he been caught, the Kazakhs would have likely killed him.

24

Knucklebones was a very popular game with us kids, no matter where we came from.

The game goes back all the way to ancient Greece and Rome. We took turns throwing actual sheep knucklebones on the ground, most of which fell flat. The kid with a bone left standing up on its side was the winner and would take all the ones that were flat on the ground.

Mostly we played the game among ourselves. Occasionally we played it with young Russian kids who weren't part of the gangs.

Not having spent our whole lives in Kazakh Republic, we were novices at the game. The Russian kids, however, were pros. As a result, they nearly always won. They won to a great measure due to a special knucklebone in their possession.

To throw a knucklebone that wouldn't fall over required great skill. But if you had a special knucklebone that was filed down with a piece of lead embedded inside, you would most likely win because, when thrown, it would almost always land standing up.

The lucky possessor of such a special knucklebone didn't just throw it, collect the losing bones, and go home. That's what you'd expect him to do, right? Wrong! That's not what he would do.

While his anxious opponent would have to patiently wait, he would perform a ceremonial routine. He'd cup the knucklebone lovingly, shake it gently, kiss it, eyes shut, mumble a prayer to the gods of chance, kiss the bone once more. Then, finally, throw it with a flourish, and only then collect the losing bones.

The special knucklebones were painted in bright reds, blues, or yellows. To this day, whenever I see a certain deep red color, it reminds me of a special knucklebone.

25

During the blazing hot summers in Turke-
stan, films were shown outdoors in an open-air theater
that was surrounded by a wooden wall. The films were
projected onto a large white screen. You had to buy a
ticket to get in. Inside, you sat on wooden bleachers.
Us kids, we had no money for a ticket. But we knew of
a hole in the wall, so we would sneak in and watch the
films for free.

Most were Russian patriotic films. After all these
years, I still remember one called *Raduga* (*Rainbow*),
which ends with a rainbow appearing in the sky after a
Soviet victory over the cruel Germans who have occupied a small village. The film is about a Russian woman
who becomes the mistress of a German officer, and her
bitter end.

I was convinced that the film was showing me the

actual events with the real people involved. I thought I was watching a documentary. Sometime later, an older boy enlightened me and said, "*Ty durachok*"—You little fool—"those are not real people; those are only actors pretending to be real people!"

What? I've been cheated all along? My cherished illusion was ripped away from me. My world fell apart! It was one of my greatest disappointments as a young kid.

26

One day, we found a small piece of film in an alley behind one of our courtyards. It was only a couple of frames. In another courtyard there was an empty storage room. The door had a small hole in the middle. We decided to have our own film screening. It was a sunny day. One of us stood outside with a mirror. He directed a reflection of sunlight into the hole. Another held the film up to the beam of light and a magnifying glass in front of the film. In the darkened storage room, we got a projection of an image on the wall that could be moved this way and that. Although the image was very blurry and it was hard to make out its contents, that was enough for us. The excitement was tremendous! A real film in a real cinema has never caused such excitement. We were so proud, as if we had just invented motion pictures.

27

Movies were rare events, so mainly we kids

made our own fun. To pass the time we loved to tell stories, especially scary stories that made your hair stand on end.

One moonless summer evening, we sat in a circle in one courtyard's darkest corner. We knew a slightly older girl who could tell scary stories like no one else.

She began her story in a normal voice.

"In a dark, dark wood"—she dragged out the word *dark*, long and slow—"was a dark, dark hill."

Her voice gradually lowered. "On the dark, dark hill was a dark, dark tombstone." She paused, the tension rising.

"Under that dark, dark tombstone was a dark, dark coffin." Now her voice was lower still. We were afraid to breathe.

"In that dark, dark coffin . . ." Here she paused again, and we were dead silent. "In that dark, dark coffin . . ." she repeated in a whisper as we leaned forward in anticipation. Then she screamed at the top of her voice: "WAS A DEVIL!"

We jumped, terrified and delighted!

As a relief from tense stories like this, we recited in unison a little nonsense rhyme we knew. We began in a normal voice:

En den deno
Sakala kameeno
Sakalaka takalaka
Tadareesa . . .

And we'd end it with a very loud "BOOM!"

At that point, worried neighbors would come out to see what the noise was. Reassured that it was only kids having fun, they would go back inside.

28

When it came time for third grade, my par-ents enrolled me in a newly formed Polish school. That marked the beginning of my scholastic confusion and a dramatic drop in my grades.

At my old school, I had become friends with a slightly older boy who was the lucky owner of a copy of *The Wonderful Wizard of Oz* in Russian. I used to go to his house and he would read aloud from the book, while I sat transfixed, eagerly swallowing each and every word.

I had to put up with his family's huge, ferocious dog. He was

chained in the middle of their walled courtyard. When I came to my friend's house, I pressed my back hard against the wall and slid sideways slowly, inch by inch, to the front door.

As soon as the dog saw me, he ran full speed to

The Polish school in Turkestan, 1945, months away from the end of the war and our departure

attack. Luckily, his chain wasn't long enough to reach
me, but I always got a terrifying display of his sharp
teeth. It took me a while to calm down. Unlike my
other neighbor's dog, regardless of how many times I
came to visit, this dog never got any friendlier.

But *The Wonderful Wizard of Oz* was such an exciting story, and I was so anxious to hear how Dorothy and her friends were doing, that no dog was going to stop me, no matter how fierce and how unfriendly.

29

One afternoon, Father closed up his shoe- repair kiosk early and rushed home to Mother and me.

"The war is over!" he exclaimed. "Hitler is dead and the Nazis are defeated." We all rushed to the market-place to listen to the radio bulletins over the speakers.

That evening, my parents began talking of going back to Poland. We'd heard plenty of stories from ref-ugees who had been in the Soviet Union since before the war and were never able to leave. My parents had no desire to spend the rest of their lives in Turkestan or in Russia. They were in a hurry to go and immediately began making plans.

I didn't want to leave. How could I leave when my Russian friend was still many pages away from the con-clusion of *The Wonderful Wizard of Oz*? How could I leave when I was dying to know if Dorothy got back home or not? I wished my parents weren't in such a rush and would give me a chance to hear the final chapters. But Mother and Father were determined and wouldn't change their minds. I was not quite ready to remain behind on my own. I had no choice. And so, to my disappointment, I would be leaving Turkestan without knowing the book's ending.

30

For three long years in Turkestan we had starved. Hunger had been our constant companion. Days followed days when we had not a bite of food. Through frigid winters and brutally hot summers, I can't recall a single night when I didn't go to sleep hungry.

During our final year and a half in Turkestan, our situation had gotten a little better, thanks to the help of Boris Mirkin and Father's artistic talent. We no longer starved and I no longer had to go to bed on an empty stomach. But life was still not easy.

Looking back, I can understand now why *The Wonderful Wizard of Oz* touched me so deeply. I can see the broad parallels between Dorothy's adventures and my life in those days.

The cyclone that tore her away from her Kansas home, that took her to a foreign land, was the Nazi blitz and the subsequent invasion of Warsaw, which tore us away from the rest of our family, chased us out of our home, and brought us to a foreign land— Belarus, Settlement Yura, and Turkestan. The wicked witches for me were Nazis, Russian hooligans, hostile Kazakhs, and hunger.

Little did I know at the time that our journey back to the west would be almost as filled with obstacles as Dorothy's return to Kansas.

31

In the Soviet Union, you needed documents giving you permission to travel. My parents decided not to wait for such permission from the authorities— to instead take a chance and leave as soon as possible.

We left our small room and moved to the train station to wait for a train.

Those were times when you didn't wait for a train for hours, but days—if you were lucky—or sometimes weeks. We even heard stories from some people that they had to wait for the right train for as long as a month.

While waiting, we slept on the station's cold, hard floor. When the train station got packed with people, there was no room to stretch out on the floor, and we had to move outside, hoping that it wouldn't rain. Outside, we slept with one eye open, because of suspicious characters hanging around, who we feared were looking for a chance to steal from us—or do even worse.

After we'd spent days at the Turkestan train station, there came a Red Cross train. It carried wounded soldiers and some regular passengers.

Father negotiated with the conductor for permission to get on the train, and after a payment of some money, we were allowed to travel while standing up in the corridor, as illegal passengers once again. And so we left Turkestan behind forever.

SIX
THE ROAD
BACK

I

For long days and nights, we traveled on the slow, overcrowded train. We were jammed in the narrow corridor with other ticketless passengers. Father, Mother, and I took turns perching on our small suitcase to give our legs a rest, but mostly we had to stand, squeezing to one side or the other if somebody wanted to pass by. Sleep was impossible. You cannot imagine how painful it was to have to stand up for so many hours, not to be able to sit down in a proper seat.

We finally stopped at a large railway station somewhere in the Russian Republic. The station had multiple tracks with many freight trains passing through.

Most of the time, the freight trains did not stop. Once in a while, a train pulling freight and passenger cars might pause, but mostly they just rolled through the station and disappeared.

While Mother and I waited at one side of the station, Father went to investigate anytime he saw a waiting train.

Then he would return and tell us that it wasn't going our way.

At the edge of the railway station were crowds of desperate-looking travelers, waiting just like us. We didn't look so great either, and it only got worse the longer we waited. Days passed. Father would hurry over when any new train arrived in the station, seeking information.

One morning, he saw a freight train marked GOMEL, the name of the town in Belarus where the theater he had worked for was based. Since that was in the general direction of where we wanted to go, he hustled back to Mother and me and we gathered our things.

When we got to that train, we found an empty freight car with one of its doors open. We climbed inside, lay down—no, collapsed—on the filthy floor, stretched out, and fell into an exhausted sleep.

Around midnight, the train left the station. After a very long ride, it came to another railway station, and there its journey ended. It wasn't Gomel in Belarus. Who knows where we were?

And so it went, on and on: endless freight trains, endless confusing train rides. After a long journey, we finally reached one of the several main railway stations in Moscow.

Moscow was hardly where we wanted to be. But as travelers without train tickets, we couldn't control our

destination. We had to accept wherever the trains took us, and that's how we ended up in Moscow, capital of the Soviet Union.

In the Soviet Union, you couldn't travel or reside in a city without legal documents, which we didn't have. We were, therefore, breaking the law: By just being in Moscow, we were criminals.

We also had the problem of how to get across town to Moscow's Kiev Railway Station—where we would find trains heading west—without arousing suspicion. To go by the underground metro was out of the question, because of possible inspections by police.

For the time being, Mother and I stretched out on a blanket on the cold tile floor of Moscow's beautiful central station, amid the noise of travelers bustling back and forth all around us.

I felt uncomfortable in the middle of all this commotion. I was afraid that someone rushing to catch a train might step on us while we were sleeping.

While Father went to find out what we should do next, Mother asked me to watch our modest possessions and went to buy food.

When she returned, she gave me a tired-looking apple along with a thin paperback with a few pictures. It told the story of an absentminded professor in a hurry who jumped into the first train car he saw, sat down, and fell asleep. When he woke up, the train hadn't gone anywhere. It had no locomotive. A modest story not entirely removed from our own situation. We, too, felt like we weren't getting anywhere.

Studying all the pictures in this little book kept me busy and was a temporary distraction from our surroundings.

While we were thus "relaxing" on the floor, Father went outside the station and stood on the street, wondering what to do. As he stood there, a municipal truck carrying garbage stopped in front of him. The driver jumped down from the cab, came over to Father, and

said, "Where to, Comrade?" Father thought perhaps he was checking for illegal travelers. The driver, seeing Father's worried expression, reassured him. Father said, "We are only passing through. We want to go to L'vov." The driver said, "Then you have to go to the Kiev Station. I can take you there for ten rubles." Apparently, he didn't mind supplementing his meager salary by making a couple of rubles on the side, even though it was illegal.

Father rode in the cab with the driver, while Mother and I rode in the back of the truck along with the trash. It was an aromatic ride through Moscow. The trash was piled all around us. I did manage to catch a passing glimpse of the magnificent Technicolor onion domes of St. Basil's Cathedral, peeking out above the mounds of trash.

When we got to Moscow's Kiev Station, we didn't smell like fresh-cut flowers. But it turned out that our transportation would only get dirtier.

2

So now we were at Moscow's Kiev Railway Station, but again, to buy tickets, we needed special documents that we didn't have. And again the station was packed with travelers who had the same problem. Everybody was equal; everybody slept on the same floor.

To make our lives more interesting, the station inspectors came periodically and told us to get up off the floor and move. Several times a day, that was our daily exercise. But as soon as the inspectors left, everybody returned to their former places.

That was not only our daily exercise, but also our main entertainment.

Father again wandered around the station for days, scouting the trains arriving at the station, looking for one that might be headed our way.

Finally he found a train marked with the eagle, the

Polish national symbol. It had brought coal to Russia and was now returning empty to the mines in southern Poland, no doubt through L'vov. When night came, we snuck our way onto the last empty coal car.

We rode for long hours on the coal-dusty floor. At long last, the train stopped at a place called Zhmerynka, a station with multiple tracks. When I caught a glimpse of my reflection in the station's window, I could hardly recognize myself. My eyes were peeking out from behind a dark mask of coal dust.

We cleaned ourselves up as best we could without a proper bathroom or running water.

3

It was the eve of the first Yom Kippur after the war. My parents decided to get off the train and rest during this holiest day of the year for Jews.

We needed fresh food supplies. While Mother and I waited at the train station, Father went to find food for us at a small village a couple of kilometers away.

When he returned hours later, carrying bread and a surprise—fruit—he told us the following story.

"When I got to the marketplace of the village, I saw a sight I hadn't seen since we left Turkestan: a profusion of fruits and vegetables. But an even bigger surprise awaited me. The market was surrounded by small wooden houses. When I got closer to them, I saw that they were the workshops of tailors, shoemakers, leather workers, just like I saw in Poland before the war. And here is the big surprise: I noticed small shop signs written in Yiddish with Hebrew letters: *Schneider*, *Schuster*, and other Jewish names. I couldn't

believe my eyes. To make sure that I wasn't dreaming, I decided to walk into a tailor's shop. I apologized for the intrusion and introduced myself. I told them I was a refugee from Warsaw, returning to Poland with my family.

"The Jewish tailor and his wife welcomed me. His

wife served me a glass of tea and some refreshments. While I drank the tea, the tailor told me how they survived the war.

"At the beginning of the war, Zhmerynka and a couple of other villages around here became part of Romania. This happened right after the Germans occupied Ukraine, where they soon set out to eliminate the Jewish population. For various reasons I don't understand, the Nazi racial laws didn't apply here. As a result, the Jews of Zhmerynka remained in their homes.

"When Jews from neighboring towns heard that Zhmerynka was safe from persecution, the village was flooded with refugees. The Germans ordered the Romanians to arrest all the newcomers. Sadly, the Jews who were not originally from Zhmerynka were all killed. The Zhmerynka Jews were the only survivors."

When Father left the tailor and his wife, he purchased a few fresh provisions at the market and returned to us with this incredible story.

4

One night, after several days at the Zhmerynka train station waiting for a new train, we snuck aboard another Polish coal train that was returning westward after delivering its ore.

Our method of transportation was not just dirty; it was downright dangerous. A government decree had gone out that travel on freight trains was illegal and subject to severe punishment.

When our train stopped at the next station, we stayed hidden in a corner of our coal car, listening to the passing footsteps of police officers checking the train.

Once our train reached Stanislavov, our hiding place was discovered. Security men took us to the police station for interrogation.

The security chief demanded, "Papers! Where do you come from and where are you going?"

Father said, "We come from Turkestan and we are on our way to L'vov. Our papers and money have been stolen."

We waited in the corridor while the chief called Turkestan to verify that we were telling the truth, and our status.

After some time, there came a man dressed in civilian clothes. By the deferential attitude of the policemen, we guessed he must be a high official. After hearing the police chief's report, he interrogated Father.

Father repeated his story and added, "No father would endanger his family by traveling thousands of kilometers without proper documents, permits, and tickets."

The high official scrutinized him, then said, "Go get tickets to L'vov. I don't want to see you again."

Here in Stanislavov, Father was at last able to get proper tickets for us, without difficulty.

And so we traveled like normal passengers, rather than stretched out on the dirty floor of a freight train or a coal car. We finally left the Soviet Union behind and came to L'vov, Poland.

5

Our Warsaw apartment had flowered wall-
paper. Because I stared at the flowers, Father named
me Uri.

Because my name was Uri, we didn't get Soviet
passports.

Because we didn't have Soviet passports, we were
sent away deep into the Soviet Union.

Because we spent the war years in faraway places
where the Nazi invasion never reached, we survived.

On the other hand, if our Warsaw apartment hadn't
had flowered wallpaper, I wouldn't have stared at the
flowers and I wouldn't have been named Uri.

If my name hadn't been Uri, we would've gotten
Soviet passports.

If we had Soviet passports, we would have

remained in Belarus, where Father had work and we had an apartment.

By remaining in Belarus, we would have been swept away by the invading Nazis and sent back to Poland to die with the rest of our family.

It goes to show that our survival had little to do with our own decisions. Rather, it was blind chance deciding our fate.

SEVEN
POLAND AND GERMANY

I

After years of exile, we had finally come back
to Poland, the country of our birth, hoping that this
would be the end of our journey.

But as we and other Polish Jews who had survived
the war in the Soviet Union discovered, many of our
fellow countrymen were puzzled and unhappy to see so
many of us Jews returning alive. Many were Poles who
had taken over residences and properties that were
owned before the war by Jews—Jews who might now
claim their property back. Then there were plenty of
others who weren't fond of Jews for their own personal
reasons. Did all Poles feel that way? No. There were
righteous Poles, who risked their lives to save Jews.

2

In L'vov, we registered with the Jewish Committee. They provided us with food and a place to sleep. Next we registered with the Polish authorities, so that now, for the first time in a long while, we had identification documents proving our Polish citizenship.

Our stay in L'vov was temporary. We remained there only for a few days. Then we took a train to Kraków. This time we traveled with legal papers.

3

When we arrived in Kraków, a disturbing story greeted us. We learned from fellow refugees what had happened only a few days earlier.

In a Kraków apartment, there were three Jewish couples, all Holocaust survivors. The three men and their wives sat at a table. To pass the time, they were playing a friendly game of cards, gambling for a few zlotys a hand.

Suddenly, there was a loud knock on the door. One of the women opened the door a crack to see who it was. A heavy boot stepped into the open crack, preventing her from closing the door. Three big Poles forced their way inside.

They ordered the women to go to another room and shut the door.

Then they shot their husbands dead in cold blood.

They didn't touch the money on the table. Before departing, they left a note: *Jews, leave Poland.*

The message was clear. In postwar Poland, Jewish life was cheap, and returning survivors were unwelcome. It wouldn't be long before my parents experienced this reality firsthand.

4

The Kraków Jewish Committee helped the returning refugees in any way they could. Their bulletin board had announcements of people searching for other family members. Nobody looked for us. Of our large family, there were no survivors in Poland. All were dead except the three of us.

5

We had no intention of remaining in an unfriendly Poland. But winter was approaching. We badly needed some rest from our long and arduous journey.

We found a small two-room apartment.

Father then met a couple with two very small boys. They were looking for a place to live. Father offered them one of our rooms. At this point, while my parents stayed in the apartment, I was placed in a Jewish children's home. It had a classroom. But instead of the lessons, I remember only the amazing stories kids told of how they survived the war.

There was one boy who stands out in my memories. He might have been at most nine or ten years old. His parents were dead, and he told hair-raising stories of how he'd traveled all alone on the roof of a train with thieves and murderers. He had to sleep with one eye open not to lose his perch and be thrown off the roof to his death. He told us of the many experiences he'd had to endure in order to survive.

We all sat transfixed in silence as he spoke. So did the teacher. He forgot to teach. This boy's telling lasted for days.

My own experiences, as painful as they had been, were not as bad by comparison, because I'd been with my parents.

One day, unexpectedly, Father showed up at the children's home and said, "Uri, we're leaving. Pack up your things quickly." As I stood there, confused about this sudden change of plans, Father urged me along. "Let's go. I'll explain as we walk." He looked upset, so I didn't ask any questions. I packed my things, and we left in a hurry. On the way, he told me what had happened.

The plumbing in the building where my parents stayed had been damaged during the war and had never been properly repaired, so the bathroom in the apartment had problems. The toilet didn't flush properly. As a solution, they kept the bathtub filled with water and used a bucket or two of water to flush away waste.

The two little boys loved to play in the bathroom, sailing paper boats and small pieces of wood in the tub. As a result of their games, something went wrong and the tub began to leak profusely and flood to the floor below.

The little boys got scared by what they had done. Instead of telling their parents, they went to their room and hid under their bed. My parents were unaware of the problem.

Suddenly, there was a loud knock on the door. It was the concierge, very upset. "What's going on here?" he shouted. "There's a flood downstairs!"

Father didn't have a chance to say a word. The concierge left in a hurry.

Now there was a loud banging on the door. The downstairs neighbor, a Polish colonel, burst in, dressed in his military uniform, loaded pistol in hand, pointing it at Father.

Father stood, frozen with fear. The colonel shouted, "You dirty Jew! You son of a bitch! I'll shoot you dead like a rabid dog. Are you trying to chase me out of my apartment so that other dirty Jews can move in?"

Father was stunned. He couldn't open his mouth.

He wondered if, after all we'd gone through to survive the war, this was going to be our end.

The colonel kept yelling. Finally Father found his voice. "Pan Colonel, no one here wants you to lose your apartment. It was an accident. The little boys, while playing, damaged the tub. Tell me how much you estimate the damage to be, and I will pay you."

Slowly the colonel lowered his gun. He went downstairs to assess the damage and came back to say, "I've recently had renovation work done. It'll cost you two thousand zlotys."

A huge sum! The colonel saw this as an opportunity to make some extra money.

While all this was going on, the parents of the little boys had gone into their room and locked their door.

Father searched his pockets, Mother searched her purse, and they came up with only a thousand zlotys. Father knocked on their roommates' door and asked for the remaining money. On the other side, silence. Not a word.

Father kept pleading with them through the door. "It's only a loan. I'll reimburse you."

Finally their door opened a crack, and a hand came out with a thousand zlotys.

After the colonel left with all the money, my parents burst into bitter sobs.

They decided not to wait for spring, as they had originally planned, but to leave Poland as soon as possible.

To repay our roommates as he had promised, Father left them a sewing machine for leather, and all the shoe-repair supplies he'd purchased in order to make a living while we stayed in Poland.

Then Father went to the Jewish Committee. He told them what had happened and asked to be registered for the next transport leaving Poland.

The clerk tried to talk him out of it. "Why not be patient, and leave in the spring? It's almost Christmas, and the trains will be full to capacity." But Father kept insisting.

Finally we were assigned to a group that was leaving, illegally, to Czechoslovakia.

The trains were packed. With great difficulty, we managed to squeeze into one of the cars.

We left Poland behind forever. Once more, we were homeless, traveling without the right papers.

6

At some point we left the train and began a long walk through the fields and forests between Poland and Czechoslovakia. We crossed the border illegally.

When we reached Bratislava, we stayed at an old hotel called Sokol. I remember the name, for some reason, but little else.

Our group of illegal travelers was led by a couple of men from Jewish Palestine. I recall nothing of the journey at this point. But I recall that when we crossed into Austria and reached Vienna, we stayed at an abandoned hospital that looked like a baroque palace. It had long, ornate, neglected corridors. In one of them I found a rusty old sword, possibly from the days of Emperor Franz Josef. Being the lucky possessor of such a sword, I marched triumphantly back and forth, up and down the corridors like a conqueror, a conqueror of empty corridors.

Although the hospital looked like a palace, it had no beds, no mattresses. When it was time for bed, we slept on the cold floor.

When we moved on from Vienna, I left the sword behind so that another lucky kid could find it and conquer empty corridors I might have missed.

After a short stay in Vienna, we traveled to southeastern Germany. We came to a DP camp—a displaced-persons camp—in Leipheim, a small town in the state of Bavaria.

The conditions were chaotic. There were many thousands of displaced, homeless, desperate refugees—survivors from death camps, survivors from the Soviet Union such as ourselves, individuals who had been hidden by gentiles, and many, many more—all of us unwanted, unwelcome people whom no country was anxious to accept.

We stayed in an empty German army barrack. Its interior was Spartan, as befits a military residence. It was lined on both sides with bunk beds. Since I considered myself a great adventurer, I chose an upper bunk. An upper bunk was more daring. I could have adventures climbing up and down whenever I wished.

My mother befriended a woman and her daughter in a neighboring barrack. The daughter was about sixteen or seventeen, a gorgeous young woman who became close to my mother. The beautiful girl wanted to trim my fingernails, and I, the great adventurer, hero, ran away from her as fast as I could. Had I been older, I would've run after her and begged, *Please, oh please, trim my fingernails as many times as you'd like!*

The beauty I ran away from instead of running after at age eleven, DP camp, Germany, 1946

7

In the Leipheim DP camp, we were given food
by the United Nations Relief and Rehabilitation
Administration. Among the provisions were Nescafé,
chocolate, and cans of meat called Spam, from America. In Turkestan, I would have given anything to eat
any kind of meat. But after a frequent diet of Spam in
Germany, I couldn't stand it.

The DP camp was near a former factory that had
made German Messerschmitt planes. There were still
some planes in disrepair parked nearby. I climbed into
one of them. As I sat in the cockpit of the plane, I
began wondering, *Could this very plane have been the one that
bombed the stairway in our building in Warsaw?* And now this
once-proud flying machine sat on the ground, helpless,
incapable of going anywhere.

8

The city of Günzburg was walking distance from Leipheim. I went there many times to see American films. I vividly remember entering the city through

an old medieval gate and walking past medieval-looking houses. To my regret, the cinema only seemed to show musicals and comedies, neither of which were favorites of mine. I wanted only action and adventure flicks.

In retrospect, I wonder if they were showing light entertainment to cheer up the viewing public after this horrible war that had only recently come to an end.

That summer, Jewish kids from the DP camp, myself included, were sent to the Bavarian Alps. We stayed in a small mountain town called Ettal.

At the camp in Ettal, there was also a group of German kids. As they waited to be served at mealtime, they sang a little refrain: *Wir leiden hunger, wir leiden hunger, / wir haben doch, so kein mal nicht gehabt, nicht gehabt.*

Yiddish is close enough to German that we Jewish kids could understand what they were saying: *We suffer hunger, we suffer hunger, / We have never had it like this, never had it like this.* They were being fed exactly like us but probably had no idea what real hunger was. We Jewish kids could have sung, *We've never had it this good, never had it this good.* The food we got there was a feast by comparison to what I'd had for years in Turkestan. For instance, it was at this camp in the mountains

Summer camp in the Bavarian Alps, Ettal, 1946

that I made my first acquaintance with a truly delicious food product from America—peanut butter. We were given slices of bread with a thin layer of peanut butter, which I only wished were thicker.

Uri at eleven and classmates, Bavaria, Germany

9

Father founded a newspaper for the residents of the Leipheim camp. Yiddish is written with Hebrew letters. Since the Nazis had destroyed all the Hebrew typefaces, the newspaper used Latin letters as a substitute. Father was the founder, editor, writer, artist, and cartoonist of the paper. He named the paper *A Heim*, which had a double meaning—it translates as both "A Home" and "To Go Home."

While Father was busy with the newspaper, I was busy decorating the wall in our barrack with paintings.

Front page of Father's newspaper, showing the masthead he designed

A newspaper caricature by Father; Mother was also an artist, as this little shell figure shows

One day, Father's newspaper photographer stopped by our barrack to take a picture of me and my art. He asked me to pose on top of my bunk bed facing my painting, as if I were in the process of working on it. Since I didn't have a real painter's palette, he asked me to hold an empty record cover as if it were a palette. When I saw the photo, I thought it looked staged and silly.

But having that photo gives me something to remember those days gone by.

Uri on top of bunk bed with one of his wall decorations, DP camp, Leipheim, Germany, 1946

10

Leipheim isn't far from Munich. One day, we discovered to our joy and amazement that my father's cousin, the artist Paul Perkal, was alive and living temporarily not far away in Munich. While he was there, he was painting decorations in an old synagogue.

He had survived the Auschwitz death camp by painting portraits of the Nazi guards. When we visited him, he gave me my first set of oil paints. That set was of particular importance to me. It meant that I had just been accepted as a fellow artist by a true professional. Besides, oil paints beat flower petals for color anytime.

Our cousin eventually moved to Australia, and to my deep sorrow I never saw him again.

I I

Thanks to his work as a journalist, Father discovered that his brother Yehiel had also survived and now lived in Paris. When we found out, we rejoiced. We had had no news from him during the war. He had survived not just World War II but also the Spanish Civil War, where he had gone to fight before I was born. That was the last Father had heard from him.

Now, when Father contacted him, Uncle Yehiel sent us a letter, asking us to come join him and his family in Paris.

I looked forward to meeting my uncle, about whom I'd heard so much.

Father as editor, the happiest period of his life

EIGHT

PARIS

I

It was the end of 1946.

We left Germany and traveled to France. We arrived in Paris at the Gare de l'Est after dark. Father's younger brother Yehiel was waiting for us at the train station.

Of four brothers, Father and Yehiel were the only survivors. The other two brothers were Moshele and Hersh.

Moshele, the youngest, died in the Warsaw Ghetto of typhoid fever.

Hersh was a brilliant religious scholar with a remarkable photographic memory. He lived in a town called Żyrardów.

When the German Nazis came to Żyrardów, they rounded up all the young Jewish men, Hersh among them. To entertain themselves, the Germans ordered them to run from Żyrardów to Warsaw, a distance of forty-four kilometers, while they rode on motorcycles.

When Hersh couldn't keep up with the other young men, the Germans shot him. He fell by the side of the road, mortally wounded. He lay there, like refuse, for a couple of days until he was rescued by death.

2

Our journey wasn't over until we took another
train to Les Vallées, a Paris suburb, where Yehiel and
his family lived.

Les Vallées bore no resemblance to Paris, but rather

to a small town. We moved in with Yehiel; his wife, Ida; their two little girls, Françoise and Evelyne; and Ida's two sisters, Silva and Edith. With the three of us, that made nine in a small apartment.

The first evening in France was a reunion celebration. Aunt Ida, with the assistance of her two sisters, had prepared a wonderful meal while Yehiel had gone to meet us at the train station. After the meal, we were all too excited to go to sleep. Instead, although it was getting late, we told about our experiences in the Soviet Union. Then it was Yehiel and his family's turn to tell about their life during the war, which they did the rest of the night.

From Yehiel, Father learned the fate of his parents. "A woman, a relative of ours who lived in France, was in touch with them at the beginning of the war, when it was still possible to send postcards," Yehiel said.

On our trip home, everywhere we stopped at night was dark. But when we reached Paris, I understood why it is called the City of Light.

"That's how she found out that our parents were in the Warsaw Ghetto."

At that time, it was still allowed to send a package weighing up to one kilogram. So she sent one kilo of tea, which could be divided into small portions and then sold for money to buy food. My grandmother wrote to say thank you, but that was the last our relation heard, according to Yehiel. The relative in Paris later learned that my grandparents had caught typhus, like many in the ghetto. When they went to the "hospital," the German doctors actually gave them injections to kill them.

Tragically, as with their sons Moshele and Hersh, their deaths were considered lucky, because the surviving ghetto inhabitants soon ended up in Auschwitz, where the death that awaited them was much worse.

3

The next day, Yehiel took Father to the Paris prefecture to register. Yehiel knew the chief clerk, and so we received legal papers without difficulty. We were now official residents of France.

Father went to work at Yehiel's tailor shop in central Paris.

When they were young kids, Yehiel had followed Father around constantly, always curious what his older brother was up to. Was he carving small rubber stamps, drawing beautiful Hebrew letters, writing articles on various subjects, or secretly wiring electricity in a closet? Yehiel had watched with admiration everything that Father was doing.

Now came a reversal of roles. Father had become an apprentice to his younger brother, who was teaching him a new profession: how to be a tailor.

4

Yehiel was very generous. He made every effort to make us feel as welcome and as comfortable as possible. Me, he treated like a son.

When Yehiel found out that I had drawn maps in the Soviet Union, he bought me a large atlas. When he learned that I collected stamps, he gave me a stamp catalog. He knew about my love of drawing, so he bought me a palette, brushes, and oil paints, in a wooden box, which could serve as a small easel.

5

One day, a few months after our arrival, brought changes in my life and the life of my parents for which I can only blame myself. This time it wasn't because of my name, as when we were refused Soviet citizenship. It was because of my action—or, rather, my inaction. My simple refusal to go on an errand. I'm not proud of it. But since this is not a work of fiction, I can't change the facts to make myself look better.

On that fateful day, I was sitting on the floor, my postage stamps spread around me. I was looking up some of them in the stamp catalog.

With stamps on my mind, I couldn't have cared less about the vegetable soup that Aunt Ida was making in the kitchen for our supper. Then she called, "Uri, take this money and go to the grocer's to buy more potatoes and onions!"

Many times before, I had been happy to go on similar errands for her. But not now.

This time I said, "No." And I went back to my stamps.

The rest of that day went peacefully, and I thought there wouldn't be any repercussions.

Was I wrong! In the evening, when Yehiel returned from work, Ida told him about my refusal to go on an errand. Reprisal came swiftly. Yehiel demanded I return all his gifts immediately. I obeyed, and I returned the atlas, the stamp catalog, and the box of oil paints.

In retrospect, I admit I should have gone on that errand. But what was done was done.

Still, to my young mind, my uncle's taking back his gifts didn't feel right either. I believed that a present should never be taken back. But it seemed now that his gifts were conditional, not fully mine, subject to be taken back at any time at his pleasure.

My refusal made waves. My impression at the

time—and perhaps I was mistaken—was that there was a slight cooling between my parents and Yehiel's family.

At any rate, my parents made two decisions. One, I must leave the house. Two, they must look for an apartment of their own in Paris.

Accordingly, my parents made inquiries for a suitable place for me. Acquaintances highly recommended a school and dorm in a small town outside Paris. I don't know if those acquaintances explained to my parents that it was a strict religious school.

But a strict religious school it was.

6

I don't remember how long I managed to endure that school. Weeks or months, my stay was too long. Praying went on all day, or so it seemed to me, when I would have preferred to draw or paint instead. At dawn, when I opened my eyes, I had to say a prayer thanking God for waking up alive. I can't remember what the evening prayer before going to sleep was about. But be assured, there must have been such a prayer for sleeping. There were also prayers throughout the day. Perhaps some seemed short for other kids. They always seemed too long to me. Then there were studies of old scriptures with tiny letters, and commentaries with microscopic ones. As a result, I soon developed eye strain and tension headaches. It became quite obvious to me that the strict life of a religious scholar wasn't for me.

Where was the fun? Where were the funny characters I loved to draw? What about comic books and
adventure stories? What about swashbuckler films?
None of them were allowed to cross the threshold of
this establishment.

I wasn't happy. No. I was miserable.

And then I fell ill.

7

I learned later that Father arrived at the
school on my birthday. He took the train from Paris,
bearing presents, and came to see me.

When he got there, the principal said, "Your son
isn't here."

Father was shocked. "Where is my son?"

"In Paris," said the principal.

"In Paris? Why in Paris?" Father asked.

"He's at the Paris children's hospital," said the principal.

Now my father was alarmed. "What? Why in the
world didn't you let us know? What is the matter with
him?"

Silence.

"What?" Father raised his voice.

Finally the principal cleared his throat and stumbled through an explanation. "Your son, um, um, came down with a sore throat and, um, um, and a high fever."

Then he was quick to reassure Father. "Oh, there is absolutely no reason to worry. We have sent word to our great rabbi in Brooklyn to pray for him."

How lucky could I get! A great rabbi in Brooklyn to pray for me!

Worried, Father rushed to the train station to take the train back to Paris. When he got there, he jumped in a taxi to the children's hospital. He was told that his son was quarantined, isolated in the infectious-diseases wing of the hospital.

He was not allowed to enter his son's room; he could only look through a glass partition. What he saw chilled his blood. I lay on my side, unconscious.

Father stood frozen in place, speechless.

After some time, the doctor came by and explained. "Your son was brought to the hospital in critical condition, with a dangerously high fever. He has diphtheria

and scarlet fever." The doctor added, "We've given him the necessary treatment. Tonight is critical. If he survives the night, there's a chance that he might make it."

In the adjoining room was a little boy with rosy cheeks who didn't look very sick.

8

Father walked the Paris boulevards to clear his mind and decide how to break the news to Mother. One look at his face and she'd know right away that something was terribly wrong. So he called his brother Yehiel and asked him to tell Mother that he'd be staying the night in Paris, under the pretext of looking for an apartment, which they still hadn't found. Then he kept walking for a long time to get as exhausted as possible. He found a cheap hotel for the night. But despite his tiredness, he had trouble sleeping and waited anxiously for morning.

Early the next morning, he took the train back to Les Vallées.

When he got home, he explained very carefully to Mother that I had been taken to the hospital with a sore throat. I was now at the hospital rather than at school, in order not to infect the other children.

Somewhat later that day, both my parents came to the hospital. On their way up to my ward, they passed an empty room with the mattress standing in the corridor. Father explained to Mother that this indicated that a patient had died and they were disposing of his mattress.

When they got to the infectious-diseases ward, Mother saw from afar a mattress in the corridor leaning against the wall. She felt a sharp stab of pain, as if a knife had pierced her heart, and she said to herself, *Uri is dead.* Father had the same thought. When they got close, Father saw that the room next to mine, the one with the little boy with the rosy cheeks, was empty. He had died during the night.

They came to my room and looked through the glass partition. I was still lying there, half conscious,

facing the wall, mumbling incoherently. All this I later learned from my parents.

My parents came every day to visit. Very slowly, my condition improved. The whole lengthy stay, I was fed only potato puree. As well as a new miracle drug: penicillin.

In one of Mother's visits, she told me that Uncle Yehiel wanted to give me back the presents he'd taken back. I refused. I had my principles.

Each time she came, she begged me to accept the presents. I kept refusing. One time she told me how much it would mean to my uncle if I'd accept them back, how deeply he felt about it, and how terribly he felt about it. I finally relented and accepted them. He never took them back again.

I used up those oil paints long ago. I still have the wooden box.

Dear reader, what saved my life? The prayers of the great rabbi of Brooklyn, or potato puree and a new wonder drug called penicillin? You decide.

9

I was brought to the hospital in February, the
month of my birth. There was snow on the ground and
the trees were bare. When I left the hospital, the trees
had begun to sprout green leaves. It was the beginning
of spring. During my stay, I'd learned how to speak
French.

I didn't go back to the religious school, nor back to
Les Vallées. In my absence, my parents had found an
apartment in Paris.

Our new apartment was in a working-class neighborhood near the Gare du Nord. It had two small
rooms and a small kitchen. The bathroom was in the
hall, to be shared by two floors. It was a Parisian squat
toilet: no seat, only a hole with a foot groove on either
side. Apartments had no showers. For that, we went to
the neighborhood public showers, where we bought a

ticket, like at the movies. In the winter, we burned coal for heating. It was no luxurious living, but it was our own apartment, and we were content.

When one of our neighbors would see me, she'd say to my mother, *"Oh, le pauvre petit, combien il a souffert."* "Oh, the poor little one, how much he has suffered."

10

Communism was popular in France in those days. We met many "easy-chair communists," as Father called them: rich people who lectured my parents about the blessings of the Soviet regime. That they had no idea what they were talking about didn't stop them from lecturing even those who had come back from the Soviet Union. We had no such illusions. We were grateful for the hospitality in the Soviet Union, which had saved our lives, but had no interest at all to live under the Soviet regime.

I I

I went to a French public school in our neigh-
borhood. When the teacher called the roll, he'd stop,
stumble, and pause as if to gather strength for a major
task. I knew he was trying to pronounce my name,
spelled the Polish way: *S-Z-U-L-E-W-I-C-Z*. He would
finally blurt out, "S-zu-lay-vyez," which bore a vague
resemblance to my name.

To my classmates, I was not *le pauvre petit*. When
it came to my name, they had none of the teacher's
difficulties. They kept it simple. They called me *sale
étranger*—"dirty foreigner."

When on occasion I was outside Paris, the local kids
called me *sale Parigot*—"dirty Parisian" in slang. So only
outside Paris did I become a Parisian. Well, perhaps
not a pure Parisian—a dirty Parisian—but a Parisian

nonetheless. Who could've guessed that to become a Parisian I'd have to go outside of Paris?

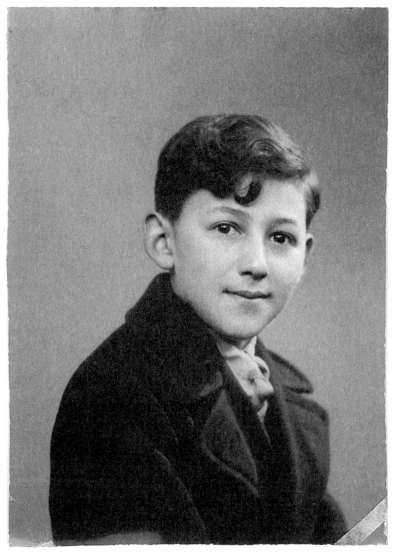

Uri in Paris, age twelve

12

In class, in our notebook, on each subject divider, we were required to draw a decorative border. Soon word got out that I was the best in our class at drawing. Therefore, my "dirty foreigner" status was temporarily suspended, and I began to get requests from classmates to draw their borders. For a time, I did it. Especially for the strongest boy, which gave me some "protection" and access to his father's newspaper store, where I could read comic books without having to buy them, which I couldn't afford to do anyway.

Drawing everybody's borders kept me quite busy, and I didn't have much time to draw well for my own borders. Finally I put a stop to this business, and I refused to draw for others. As a result, my *sale étranger* status resumed. Soon, during class breaks I began to get challenged to boxing matches.

I was good with a pencil, but bad as a boxer. Somehow I managed to have the upper hand with one classmate, who was an even worse boxer than I was. Next time, no such luck. I lost badly. The result was a bleeding, broken nose.

I was desperate to improve my fighting skills. There was no one to help me. Father knew nothing of boxing. Neither did any of our family's male friends. I grew up in a world where fighting skills were a mystery, a gift from God—you either had them or not, period.

A nice break from the fighting matches came when our teacher read us a story by Edgar Allan Poe, "The Murders in the Rue Morgue," translated by the French poet Charles Baudelaire, a great admirer of Poe. We sat, listening, in stunned silence.

13

I was chosen to represent our school in a drawing competition between all the schools of our Paris district. When drawing, I was in my element. Drawing was my pleasure. I'd been drawing all my life, since I was able to hold a pencil and decorate the wall near my crib with scribbles.

At the competition, we were given paper, pencils, and paints. Our assignment was to portray a kid selling newspapers on the street. I did my best, then handed it in to the art teacher and went home.

Sometime later, when I came to school, I was told that I won first prize. That was my first art honor. As a boxer I was a loser, but when it came to drawing, I was a winner. My award was a kid's version of *Gulliver's Travels*. I would have been much happier with a book of swash-buckling cape-and-sword stories or a comic book. But a kid's version of *Gulliver's Travels*? Please . . . I was also given a savings-account booklet for two hundred francs.

Two hundred francs wasn't a fortune. But almost fifty years later, I rediscovered the bankbook and went to the bank to redeem my prize. With the interest accumulation, I expected it to have grown into something

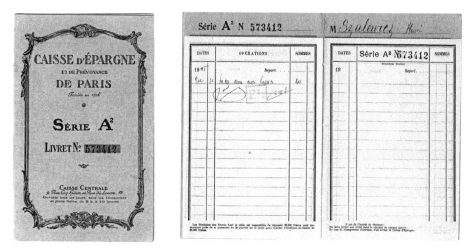

Savings book for first prize in a drawing contest

far more substantial than the initial two hundred francs. When I presented the booklet to the clerk, she said, "So sorry, it has expired. You've come too late." And so I was left with a small passbook, beautifully handwritten, but not worth a centime.

A selection of my drawings from my time in Paris. At school, I
adopted the French name Henri and spelled my name the Polish way.

14

You can't survive a war and come out scot- free. An X-ray showed that I had spots on my lungs. I wasn't sick enough to go to a sanatorium, but I wasn't healthy enough to neglect my lung problem either. I was sent south to a preventorium in the French Pyrenees mountains, in the countryside near a small village called Gelos, not far from the city of Pau and the Spanish border. It was a place for Jewish kids with health problems similar to mine.

My experience there was unlike my experiences at other children's homes. I liked the other kids and the staff. In a word, I was happy. I stayed there half a year.

My French improved. I learned many French folk songs. Many years later, I used one of them to create a picture book, *One Monday Morning*.

I read many French books, among them translations

of Jack London's *White Fang* and *Call of the Wild*, which were very popular with young people in France.

I left the preventorium when my lung spots were calcified. I have lived with them this way ever since.

Uri, age twelve, at preventorium, Southern France, near Pau

15

Back in Paris, I returned to the French school.

I was crazy about comic strips. I waited impatiently for the weekly publication of my favorite magazine, *Coq Hardi* (*Brave Rooster*), and especially the weekly installment of *Le Capitaine Fantôme* (*The Phantom Captain*), a graphic novel about pirates.

I drew pictures for a pirate comic strip of my own. Roger, one of my classmates, wrote the captions, because his printing was better than mine, and so was his French. In my youthful arrogance, I thought my masterpiece was ready for publication. It was my baby. Roger and I schlepped to the end of Paris, to the editorial office of *Coq Hardi*.

Monsieur Marijac, the editor, took one quick look at our work. Perhaps he thought, *Oh, it's one of those . . .* I don't know what he thought, because at first he said

*My pirate comic strip was lost, but here is my attempt at thirteen to create a graphic novel
from* The War of the Buttons *by Louis Pergaud*

nothing. Instead, he pulled out a blank sheet of paper, took his fountain pen, and drew a pirate. He showed it to me and said, "That's how you draw a pirate," and gave me his drawing. Perhaps another kid would have been happy with a drawing by the master. Well, I was not. I said nothing and we left. I carried the drawing, as well as my rejected masterpiece. I was deeply disappointed and angry. I hadn't come all that way to get a lesson on how to draw a pirate. Months later, I tore up the editor's drawing.

My work with Roger soon ended. I expected him to be my friend as well as my collaborator. When my classmates turned against me once more, I was deeply disappointed when Roger joined them.

I wanted a friend my age. A true friend. Not a "friend" like Roger. If I couldn't have a true friend, I'd rather be alone. And alone I was.

But not for long. Soon I made new kinds of friends. Now that I was alone, I had more time, and I read books every chance I had. Especially books by Alexandre Dumas. They were historical novels, filled with action, drama, and excitement. I read many of his books, and since most of his novels had five or six volumes, I ended up reading thousands of pages. They gave me many hours of pleasure. And so Monsieur Dumas became my friend. True, he didn't know it, but I didn't care. I knew that Alexandre Dumas was my friend, and that was enough.

Around that time, I started a small notebook, a kind of personal encyclopedia of writers and their books. The first writer I included was, of course, Monsieur Dumas. I drew his likeness, and I wrote down when and where he was born, as well as the titles of some of his books. In due time, my notebook became as well a list of my circle of friends.

Alexandre Dumas took me on fascinating journeys through French history. That is how I met D'Artagnan and his *Three Musketeers* friends, Athos, Porthos,

Notebook entry for Alexandre Dumas père (father) and his playwright son, Alexandre Dumas fils

and Aramis. They were an elite guard in service to the king, to protect him and the queen from the plots of his minister, Cardinal Richelieu. As I later found out, the characters of D'Artagnan and his friends were based on real people who had lived four hundred years ago. The real D'Artagnan served the king with distinction all his life. When the books came to an end, D'Artagnan and his friends kept living in my mind.

As my journey through Dumas's books continued, I met the mysterious Count Alessandro Cagliostro, who may or may not have been a count. He made many claims: that he was two thousand years old, that he had magical powers, that in Egypt he had studied alchemy, the art of transforming lead into gold. In Paris, he became a sensation when news spread that he had conjured the apparition of Queen Marie-Antoinette in a carafe of water. Although I didn't include him in my circle of friends, I couldn't forget him either.

Then Dumas introduced me to the future Count of Monte Cristo, Edmond Dantès. When Edmond Dantès was set to become the youngest captain of a ship, and about to marry his sweetheart, the happiest day of his life turned into the worst day of his life. He was unjustly condemned and thrown into a dungeon cell in the notorious Château d'If, a fortress prison from which no one had ever escaped, built on a small, rocky island surrounded by the dangerous currents of the Mediterranean Sea . . . How could Dantès ever escape such a tomb and become the Count of Monte Cristo?

With stories such as these, is it surprising that I fell under Alexandre Dumas's storytelling spell?

Although Dumas had written many books, at some point I was unable to find any I hadn't read. In the meantime, I discovered additional writers of swashbuckling books. One of them was Paul Féval. Thanks to him, I met another exciting character, the Chevalier de Lagardère, a master swordsman, the exclusive possessor of the invincible hidden technique of the secret sword thrust. *Bad guys! Watch out! Lagardère is coming!*

Oh, how I wished I knew of a secret boxing punch. If I'd had such a skill, I would have challenged my hostile classmates: *Come on, I'm ready for you!*

I added Paul Féval to my circle of friends. I also included in my notebook writers whose books I hadn't read yet. They were candidates waiting to become my friends. So much for being alone . . .

Last, but very far from least, was my faithful friend, who had never betrayed me—drawing. Drawing enabled me to create worlds, real or fantastic; characters, funny or sad, young or old; streets or cities, mountains or oceans. If I could create such worlds, how could I ever be lonely?

16

When it came to movies, I was very broad-minded. I loved them all. Well, as long as they had swashbucklers, pirates, cowboys, or cloak-and-dagger action. Provided, of course, the actors didn't begin to sing instead of talk.

I had no patience for singing characters. As a kid, I considered them to be wasting their time and mine, when instead they could have been acting in an adventure. Now they can sing all they like.

Television didn't exist. I depended on what the movie houses had to offer. I had no such thing as a steady allowance, so on that happy occasion when I got pocket money for a movie, it was vital that I find the right film.

If I couldn't find the right film, I'd settle for Charlie Chaplin's silent comedies, or Laurel and Hardy talkies.

I walked hundreds of blocks, checking all the movie houses, studying the posters and still photos beneath the marquees. When I finally decided on a movie, I would watch it three, four times to savor it as long as possible—and to imagine that the movie was longer than it was.

One day, after walking for blocks and blocks in search of a film, I was getting tired. That's when I made a fateful mistake. I invested my couple of francs—my hope and confidence in the film I was about to see—in a ticket. But . . . oh, what a disappointment that was! It was the Marx Brothers making fun of the Three Musketeers. The Three Musketeers were my friends! I took it as a personal offense.

Most of the time, though, I enjoyed whatever movie I'd chosen.

When I entered the cinema, it was day; when I left, it was dark. The bright Paris lights were dancing, my head was spinning, and I walked home happy.

Sci-fi graphic sequence drawn at thirteen

17

My favorite hangouts were the stalls of the

bouquinistes—the booksellers—along the River Seine.

I'd walk up and down the quai, looking at the books. Some of the booksellers sold coins going back to the French Revolution, coins still bearing the head of Louis XVI, before he lost it courtesy of the guillotine and Robespierre.

On happy occasions, when I had a few francs, I'd buy a book or a couple of old coins.

I spent so much time walking back and forth along the book stalls that I got to know many of the booksellers and they got to know me. We began to exchange greetings like old acquaintances: *"Bonjour, monsieur."* *"Bonjour, jeune homme."* "Good day, sir." "Good day, young man."

18

We lived in France, mostly in Paris, for two
and a half years, from 1946 to 1949. In 1949 I was
fourteen years old. The state of Israel was one year
old. Father was anxious to emigrate there as soon as
possible. Mother wanted to extend our stay in Paris.
She pleaded with Father, "What's the hurry? We hear
of shortages of food and housing in the newly established state. Here in Paris, we have an apartment; you
have work. Why not stay longer and rest? After all our
travels, deprivations, constantly moving, why rush?"
Mother was making a perfectly reasonable argument.
But Father argued, "Wait? Go when I'm old? It'll be
too late. No. Let's go now."

My Paris experience meant a great deal to me, and
I was grateful for it. But I hadn't felt welcome, mostly,
having been called "dirty foreigner." So I agreed with

Father that we should leave France and go to Israel. Mother was outvoted.

In August 1949 we emigrated.

I lived in Israel for ten happy years. After studying art in Israel, I yearned to continue my studies abroad. America to me was only a land of dreams and of movies. When my cousins invited me to come to New York City to study art, it was a generous offer I couldn't refuse. And so, to my surprise, I moved to New York in 1959. I was twenty-four years old.

I had no plans to stay. But life had other plans.

I'm now an old man, and I'm still here. After years of travels, I now only travel in my books.

Mother in Israel, after the war

Afterword

When my father was approaching the last decade of his life, he taught himself how to use a computer. Then he proceeded to write his memories of the war years.

He printed them from his computer, then bound them into a slim volume of about half a dozen copies, which he titled *To There and Back*.

I'm most grateful to him for making this effort as he was nearing the end of his life. His account, combined with my own memories, constitutes the foundation of my book.

Although I have a pretty good memory, and I'm amazed how much I still remember about what happened over eighty years ago, naturally I've forgotten things as well.

Father's book was invaluable in providing details of what I didn't remember and about events at which I wasn't present, such as his encounter with the Polish colonel. Some of Father's memories I remember well because he told them to Mother and me. I even remember a detail he seems to have forgotten, which struck me as important—his purchase in Dzhambul of a brochure with the picture of Lenin. And then there are instances of events at which I was very much present but incapable of remembering a thing, such as being unconscious at the Paris hospital.

My thanks to my wife, Paula Brown. Whenever I'd recount some of my memories, her probing questions compelled me to dig deeper and helped me to remember more.

My thanks to my former editor of many years, Margaret Ferguson, with whom I worked on *How I Learned Geography* and *When I Wore My Sailor Suit*—my two picture books based on memories from my childhood, which led me to this book.

Thanks also to designers Aram Kim and John Daly; copy editor Karen Sherman; production editor Allyson Floridia; my longtime friend and partner in the production department, Susan Doran; and the rest of the FSG team.

Last, but very far from least, I'm grateful to my editor, Wesley Adams, for his hard work and diligence and for being instrumental in making this the best possible book.

In memory of my parents

Farrar Straus Giroux Books for Young Readers
An imprint of Macmillan Publishing Group, LLC
120 Broadway, New York, NY 10271

Copyright © 2020 by Uri Shulevitz
Map copyright © 2020 by Gene Thorpe, Cartographic Concepts, Inc.
All rights reserved
Printed in the United States of America by LSC Communications,
Crawfordsville, Indiana
Designed by Aram Kim
First edition, 2020

1   3   5   7   9   10   8   6   4   2

mackids.com

Library of Congress Cataloging-in-Publication Data is available.

ISBN: 978-0-374-31371-5

Our books may be purchased in bulk for promotional, educational, or business
use. Please contact your local bookseller or Macmillan Corporate and
Premium Sales Department at (800) 221-7945 ext. 5442 or
by email at MacmillanSpecialMarkets@macmillan.com.